GEORGE MEREDITH
born 12th February 1828
reproduced from a photograph by permission of Mr Frederick Hollyer.

ASPECTS OF GEORGE MEREDITH

ASPECTS OF GEORGE MEREDITH

By
RICHARD H. P. CURLE

WITH A PORTRAIT AFTER THE PAINTING BY G. F. WATTS

"Our new thoughts have thrilled dead bosoms."—
The Pilgrim's Scrip.

PHAETON PRESS
New York
1970

Originally Published 1908
Reprinted 1970

Published by PHAETON PRESS, INC.
Library of Congress Catalog Card Number 72-91349
SBN # 87753-012-2

To
R. L. W.

Preface

I HAVE to thank Mr Meredith for his very great kindness in allowing me to use such quotations from his works as I required. I need hardly say that he has not read the proofs of this book and cannot be held in any way responsible, even through the most negative attitude of implied consent, for a single remark throughout.

I have also to thank certain friends who have given me great help in reading both the MS. and the proofs, and suggesting many alterations and modifications of a valuable description.

Finally, I would like to acknowledge my indebtedness to that considerable army of authors who have produced either books, pamphlets, or articles on Mr Meredith and his works, and whose many suggestive remarks are helping to build up a real body of criticism around these novels and poems. Although I have quoted but slightly from the words of others, I have diligently read and noted much that has been written on the subject.

R. H. P. C.

Contents

CHAP.		PAGE
I	GENERAL INTRODUCTION TO THE STUDY OF GEORGE MEREDITH:	
	(I) Novelist	1
	(II) Poet	15
II	MEREDITH'S PERSONALITY EXPLAINED BY ATMOSPHERE AND STYLE	27
III	PHILOSOPHY OF NATURE	56
IV	LYRICAL VIEW OF NATURE	81
V	PHILOSOPHIC CONCEPTION OF SOCIAL PROBLEMS	105
VI	INSIGHT INTO CHARACTER	119
VII	ON TRAGEDY	164
VIII	ON DEATH	184
IX	ON LOVE	197
X	ON EGOISM, SENTIMENTALISM, AND THEIR RELATIONSHIP	216
XI	THE COMIC SPIRIT	229
XII	SENSE OF HUMOUR	243
XIII	AS APHORIST AND METAPHORIST	258
XIV	THE ELOQUENCE OF MEREDITH	272
XV	LAST WORDS ON CRITICISM, METHOD, AND SOME OMISSIONS	288

ERRATA.

Page IX, *after last entry insert* INDEX 303
,, 9, line 17, *for* , *read* ;
,, 24, line 12, *for* Nature *read* nature
,, 47, line 15, *for* Feveral *read* Feverel
,, 59, line 17, *for* her *read* Her
,, 62, line 1 of text, *for* is *read* are
,, 75, line 12 of text, *for* to *read* of
,, 76, line 12, *insert* , *after* sun
,, 78, line 12 of second quotation, *insert* . *after* sank
,, 78, line 13 of second quotation, *for* . *read* ,
,, 84, line 7 of text, *for* poor *read* prose
,, 88, line 2 of first quotation, *delete* —
,, 93, line 6 of quotation, *insert* . *after* unrevealed
,, 94, line 8 *for* react *read* act
,, 101, line 5 of text, *for* night *read* might
,, 110, line 13, *for* , *read* .
,, 110, line 19. *for* . *read* ,
,, 112, line 20 of text, *for* opinions *read* opinion
,, 128, line 10, *delete* ,
,, 145, line 9 of quotation, *after* none *insert* ,
,, 165, line 21, *for* catastrophy *read* catastrophe
,, 170, line 13, *for* Rosamond *read* Rosamund
,, 171, line 2 of text, *insert* a *before* woman
,, 178, line 12, *for* These *read* There
,, 186, line 24, *after* creations *insert* .
,, 278, line 18, *for* his *read* this
,, 280, line 4 of text, *for* Guidescarpi *read* Guidascarpi
,, 280, line 10 of text, *delete* ,
,, 292, line 24, *for* the *read* he
,, 304, *insert fresh entry*, Comic Spirit, The, 15, 42, 229, 232, 236, 238, 241, 299
,, 305, *insert fresh entry*, Didacticism, 25, 83, 298
,, 305, *after Hymn to Colour, The,* quoted 62 *insert* ; explanation of, 62
,, 308, *insert fresh entry*, Paradox, Numbing effect of, 264
,, 309, *insert fresh entry*, Selincourt, Mr. Basil de, 62 *N*.
,, 309, *after* Trevelyan, Mr. G. M., 43, 58, 61 (quoted) *insert* , 62 *N*.

CHAPTER I

General Introduction to the Study of George Meredith

I. Novelist

SOME time ago, a certain number of people, becoming tired of the polite and tender sentiment which pervaded the novels of the day, began to call out loudly for more realism. They informed us that their desire was for life, not for idealism. But having had their wish granted, they began, not the less loudly, to proclaim that realism was disgusting and degrading. And so the question is one that is bound to arise, ' What is the correct attitude of the novelist in these present days of acute mental introspection ? ' Idealism [1] is transparently a playing with

---

[1] Of course, when idealism and realism are used, it is in a purely popular sense, and what is more, in a sense of such definite contrast as will strongly throw into relief their differences. Naturally enough no novelist falls conclusively into either class (for instance, there is not a sadder writer than Turgenieff—there is not one more filled with the spirit of spring and youth and love), but for the sake of the meaning, we may assume the general inclination to be the same thing.

emotions rather than a presentation of them. Realism tends to an unhealthy survey of gross and morbid sensations. Here are the two extremes: the idealist, whose mind is fixed on acquiring knowledge of what the world ought to be; the realist, who is burrowing beneath the surface, for knowledge of what the world is.

The true idealist is not one who demands peculiar situations. His idea of humanity is of the embracing mind. Wave the wand, he says, and you will find us all covered with the film of romantic idealism. His error is, that he cannot tell us whether this be true as things stand, or whether it be true as they ought to stand. For a study of the idealist's methods does not reveal to us who is to blame for the present trend of the universe in general, nature or ourselves. It is a point of no little importance; for in the one case we may treat him as a prophet, in the other as a reformer. But there is question as to the actual desirability of his aims. The position of the idealist may be challenged. He attempts to regulate humanity in particular, as it is regulated in general. He fails to grasp one of the greatest truths of life, that passion will make every man an exception to his own actual view of humanity. For a great paradox is apparent in all of us : we feel that we are advancing towards something higher, whether we believe in immortal life or the ethical future of man; and we know that it is the irresistible purpose of our life, and yet passion makes the present the one imperative call on our innermost soul, blotting out all hopes and fears, all regrets, philosophies, denials, that we may *now* live. In reality we are following nature's means to her end ; we think we are gaining our own end. The strange conflict between flesh and spirit is here laid aside and they are joined together. This is the region unexplored in the idealist's philosophy.

Now, on the other hand, the realist asserts that he has placed his hand upon the very pulse of existence. Civilization, he says, is merely a gloss, thrown over animalism. If we are to understand the motives that govern life, let us cast all sentiment aside, and searching the heart itself, realize that each separate life is entirely egoistical. The ferocious fight of hunger and desire has absolute possession of the realist's mind. Bitterness, tragedy, death, he proclaims, are our common heritage. He does not convince, because he is too obviously material. The soul is to him merely the elevated mind of a beast, innately governed by cunning and brutality. Though he does not know it, he is of all pessimists the most pessimistic. His very use of the word 'innately', as applied to the soul, explains it. Here and there, it is true, he catches glimpses of a conscience rising superior to its soul, but it is the exception, and indeed the position is impossible. He is a fatalist, with no gleam of light. He is the mental counterpart of that hopeless remark, 'Eat, drink, and be merry, for to-morrow we die.'

In the idealist's case the ethical spirit is shrouded by the sentimental, in the realist's by the material. The mistake of both is in allowing their view of life to be governed by the emotions alone, rather than by a mixture of brain and emotions. Once let the sense of proportion be clouded, and caricature, unintentional and mirthless, is bound to appear.

And this touches close upon the question of the actual art of these two schools. In an obvious way, and in a way that is not so obvious, thought sways and governs expression. It is also true, however, that expression is the medium through which thought convinces or fails to convince. But let us note this point ; they both spring from a common source —the same brain, and consequently they are seldom, if ever, out of proportion to one another. The expression has the same attributes and the same faults as the thought. The idealist encloses his dreams in the delightful frame of romantic sentiment. This is true of style and language. The realist, intent upon the exposure of frailty and sadness, uses words in the same gloomy and foreboding spirit, which darkens all his outlook. His methods lack the essential lightness of the stylist. The true buoyancy of the old, great writers, is, indeed, wanting to both ; for one lives in the atmosphere of the hothouse and the other in the atmosphere of the garret. They press nature into their service. Her voice is to them but the echo of the human cry. They fail to comprehend that man is only a part of nature, and that nature is not a brainless force, to be guided by man. Because she takes no account of individuality, they say that she is cold ; because her workings are impersonal, they say that they are without direction.

Curiously enough, there is, in reality, no

difference in the idealist's and the realist's view of nature. To both, she is merely the background of their sensations. As their minds change, she is bright or dark, but in herself she entirely lacks an individual philosophy. They will, indeed, seek gladness or comfort in her, but it is with the thought, ' You are unchanging, you are always happy ', or ' You do not suffer, you are for ever calm '. It is the negative appeal of death, not the positive appeal of life. They could not understand that passionate cry, ' Earth makes all sweet '.[1] To that writer she is the living mother, to them she is merely the mirror of their own souls. The sanest and most splendid quality, which goes to form the greatest minds, is, after all, the sense of harmony. Gulfs, differences, contrasts are the superficial formation of existence ; beneath the surface, as the sea beneath her waves, all is order, sequence, gradation. This is the scheme of nature.

We can now, indeed, actually ask the question, ' What is the correct attitude of the novelist ? ' We have expelled, in turn, the idealist and the realist, but it is becoming noticeable, that we have only started upon

[1] *One of our Conquerors*, chap. xlii.

another circuit of the same circle. The point to be raised is of a middle course, along which the novelist of the future will travel. Study of our few, great latter-day novelists will give us our answer—the observation of types of humanity. It is what they demand and what they have endeavoured to present. On the extreme of one hand is the path of the idealist, on the extreme of the other the path of the realist, and in the middle is the road of the novelist of types. Let us examine clearly the meaning of this expression. Philosophy, he says, is the foundation of all knowledge of humanity ; psychology is the key to character and the herald of the future. The study of individuals, he adds, is the study of eccentricity and exception. The germ of individual individuality in each destroys the perspective of unalterable laws. For every man tries to become a law to himself, though collectively he is seen upon the one unmistakable track. The methods of the novelist of types are founded upon nature's methods ; she works impersonally, he also. Human nature will, he says, like nature, evolve from general laws. His object is to lay bare these laws, that underlie not only life but individuality itself. For, he remarks, an exception is only an exception because it is by itself and unexplainable. In reality it is the outcome of an ordered sequence. He claims that careful observation will throw open to the light the inmost secrets of human action and thought. For his view of the novel is a serious one. He is as much out of sympathy with the man who tries simply to picture the obvious surface-life of the world around him, as he is with the idealist or the realist.

Greek sculpture presents what is possibly the acme of perfection of the type in art. That sense of calm omniscience dwells in a feeling of ageless perfection, which so grandly bodies forth the spirit of the universal and enables us to realize the faculty of changelessness.

To the novelist of types the novel is indeed the most accurate and convincing medium for philosophy. As philosophy exists for the benefit of mankind, if it be only to point the truth, will it not, he says, be more realizable, if it be shown subtly working in actual human lives? His characters are people who have never walked this earth. They are compounds of the characteristics of their various classes. Nevertheless they are not dead, for to each he gives the characteristic individuality of the class. There is about them an air of etherealized flesh and blood. At times they may appear unreal; they are never caricatures. They are types. Through them, he watches the influences at work that build or destroy: through them, his hand is upon the throb of impulse which is individuality, and the beat of fate which is fundamental law. In each of his figures is summed up the essence of a mass of humanity. Inconsistencies of character are shown to be the consistency in one class, strange gleams of thought, the heaving battle of advancement in another. He claims insight into our million indefinable emotions. The tortured and goaded soul is not led by laws of chance, he says, it is led by laws of certainty. Once understand the workings of these laws, and we know, not only the cause of ruin and disaster, but the cure also, or rather the prevention. Humanity, in the midway between nature and civilization, has lost the centre of control. It is his work to regain it, and to make the balance surer than before.

Now it may have been assumed, that such a position at the outset, is, of necessity, one of absolute impartiality; that he is, in fact, the complete philosopher. It is true and yet it is not altogether true. He is innately, and by training, an optimist. A voice within him and the teaching of science tell him that we are rising. Whence, whither, are not the vital questions with him. He is wise enough to know that they have no human answer. He believes this; that on the sweep of broad and to some extent incomprehensible lines the workings of nature are good. His metaphysics pave the way to his ethics. Therefore he cannot be said to be absolutely impartial. But the partiality is certainly in his soul, so his position could not well be otherwise. He comes to his task with a more kindly eye for humanity, than a strictly impartial one. Underneath everything, he says, there is the spark of our common brotherhood: if you seek, you will find it. Our sins and frailties, he remarks, are not those of darkness, they are those of humanity as it is. But it does not prevent him from seeing them, nor indeed from rating them soundly. He is convinced that, on the whole, humanity is upon the upward path. Thus it is that his psychological study of us tends to show the world governed by motives where not actually good, at least exceedingly human. But it is not the less keen and clear

—there are those, undoubtedly, who would say that it was only the more so.

Again, he is not the complete philosopher (who is bloodless) because he is at the same time a poet and a humorist. The three essentials in the mind of the novelist of types are, he says, philosophy, poetry, humour. Philosophy shows him the way of reason and enquiry, poetry points to him the oneness of nature and humanity, humour gives to him the sense of proportion. They are imperceptibly welded together in his soul. They make him sage, yet keep him human; they make him poetical, yet keep him sane.

And now we are to consider a point in the outlook of the novelist of types, which is, perhaps, the most illuminating point of all. We have seen that he bases all profound knowledge of life on a dexterous reading of types. There is a question which has very probably come forward, ' How does he form a type, and what are his reasons for supposing it correct ? ' For once, there is suspicion of the accuracy of his basis, he teaches to deaf ears. All philosophies are tentative, and so every one may, and probably will, convince some one : facts are concrete and must be accounted for. You may play with them, but if you are found out, you are doomed. Ever since the world began, one of the most fatal things to progress has been sound reasoning upon an unsound basis. Religions have lived and grown for thousands of years on it; for if we allow the foundation truths of any religion, the rest is entirely logical. And it is the same with all intellectual questions and all assumed positions.

It is very necessary that his methods should be made clear. His argument is one of simplicity. Each separate individual is to himself, he says, a type. In his own mind he represents a class. But it is not possible for the observer to form a type from one personality, because alone, he appears to the outsider (who cannot really distinguish between rule and exception) a mountain of individual eccentricity. Nevertheless, read from the inside, he is no exception, but a type. The plan of the novelist of types is to place himself mentally in the position of each one of his characters. For, he remarks, we can only work in the interior of one mind—our own. All other souls are in truth but the mirage of each soul. We understand them, in so much as they are reflections of ours. Even then the grasp holds but a fraction of their significance. In other words, we spread the glow of reality over the rest, it is not blown from them to us. He claims that as things are he is in the best position to put himself in the minds of others. His qualities are those that give him the completest possible human insight and sympathy. Besides this, he is able to escape the influence of actual passions, though he sees it and can follow its track. He becomes a dual individuality to watch his own soul in the positions he places it in, working out the problems of separate destinies and classes. He does not by any means force the action of his mind; his method is to let it follow the natural course of a certain kind of mind, placed in certain circumstances. He is like a doctor, who is attending to a case and at the same time taking notes of it. Actual observation of humanity, he indeed considers of importance, but it is mainly with the idea of gaining that rudimentary and essential knowledge of mankind which must act as a keystone to all conjectural knowledge. For instance, he would very largely claim that insight into one human being, gained from actual observation, would put him in possession of a mind capable of realizing the outlook of the rest of humanity.

Even individual eccentricity, as we have said before, seems to him governed by actual laws; therefore capable of innate mental comprehension. He means that not only would he be able to account for it in a chance character, but that if he himself had been forming that character from his own mind, it would still have displayed the same eccentricities. Though each human being, he says, is born with something no one else has ever had, that something is just as much the result of laws and as much subject to them as the commonest trait. Besides this, the progress of humanity is not merely the result of individual individuality, but also of the individuality of the race, the individuality of nature's law. Nothing, says the novelist of types, is an exception; many things are unknown.

Finally, we come to the last point of his outlook. We must clearly understand that he claims the vantage ground of the spirit of aloofness—which has been called the comic spirit. He views us all from a height, and therefore he views us all together, and all at the same time. He sees influences at work which are unknown to the actors themselves; he sees fate's slow, vast sweep, which can be observed only from above the tempestuous fight ; he sees the mysterious sixth sense, which sways mankind with sympathetic movements. The intense grip of life's gigantic panorama prevents his view from becoming warped. The comic spirit is the smile of infinity on the efforts and yearnings of finity : it is the look of eternity on time.

These then are some of the aims that he has set before himself ; collectively they may be said to represent the outlook of the novelist of psychology.

II. Poet

Close definitions of poetry are notoriously unsatisfactory to all but the makers. Descriptions of scenery, for instance, do not give to all the readers of it similar emotions. We must remember that there are two personalities to be considered, the personality of the watcher and the personality of the land. Nature holds more tremendous meanings for some than for others, and also more tremendous meanings in some places than in others. They act and re-act on one another. This man feels that he is happy where spread seas of tropical warmth, that one where lie keen and frosty fields of snow. Each one feels that here his inmost soul is personified, that here nature and he become personal to one another. Thus to every man, whether it be the Southern Cross, or the traffic in the city, that most thrills him (and there are examples of both), there is in that spot the heart of life, of nature.

Now we begin to see from this, two rules which should guide us in attempting to make even the broadest, which are perhaps the only safe, definitions of poetry.

First, to remember that poetry is the highest expression of personality on subjects themselves outside the boundaries of exact explanation. In the entrancing music of heaven there are notes infinitely fine, haunting, suggestive. One man in ten thousand hears, like the voice of the wild swans, that, in the mists of evening, pass by as from the uplands to the sea with tragic and mysterious cries, a melody never heard before. In a moment he is beyond philosophy : science and experience sink to nothingness. This faint music is the gate of immortal thoughts. Suddenly things assume proportions—death and life melt into one, time and space are no longer separate. He is divinely intoxicated, that is to say, he is full of convictions utterly unexplainable in positive words. The message of the night is something beyond an academic certainty to him, it is something on which he can found all his ideas of life. Yet put into words his case fails, and he is either the dreamer, the poet, or the mystic. To him romance and beauty have the indefinite definity of eternity. They are to him the spirit of the rolling years, the spirit of the endless song of nature. Actual poetry, then, must be comprehended as speaking to such senses, and close dogmatism will show a lack of this comprehension.

Secondly, to remember that we must assume a certain mental power in the definer. Every one who makes a definition of poetry is to a certain degree right, for in so far as he can, he has expressed what it means to him personally. His brain and his imagination have given him in greater or less degree that transcendental vision which is the soul of the poet. And everyone has made or is capable of making this definition. For as we have said, it is a matter of the re-action of personalities. Every man has his personality, and of course nature has her million personalities. The spirit of poetry is innate in everyone, and it is just for this very reason that we demand a certain intellectual standard in the definer of it. Otherwise we shall before long arrive at the unprofitable argument of whether there is such a thing as taste, or why everyone's opinions should not be of equal weight. The demand is not really an assumption, because, realizing the universality of the spirit, we must see that it will certainly appear in every degree of latent and half awakened sensibility. The uneducated and stupid read into conventional words, images and thoughts, in themselves divine and inexpressible, or rather, they are as much so to them as the deepest thoughts of the genius are to him. It is all a matter of proportion. The thoughts indeed are not so grand as the thoughts of the genius, but even so, the language that expresses them, is not adequate to them. Your half-educated person who remarks 'The moon is lovely' does not perhaps feel profoundly on the subject, but certainly infinitely more profoundly than you would suppose from these words. The highest flights of poetry, also, are but the faintly heard notes of a grander choir. However noble or however feeble may be the thoughts of those who look at the stars, remember one thing—they are

STUDY OF GEORGE MEREDITH

looking at the stars. This in itself is a point for thought.

And again the artistic sense is in some degree subconscious. One facet of it may be organically trained, while the others lie dark and lifeless. People of natural ability and little artistic training or education can feel acutely the beauty of starry nights and autumn woods, and yet have the most elementary taste in actual poetry. Some people who love the country will stroll out in the evening to hear the wild cries of grouse upon the sleeping moorland or the pheasants calling in the darkening woods. They will listen entranced—filled with the strange romance of the night. But many of these people are in no sense literary. There are men who will watch a sunset sinking deeply on the sea and realize in a flash that there is something more there than the mere waste of waters—suddenly they dream a dream of splendour. But many of these will never read a line of poetry. Examples of such a kind are capable of endless expansion. The meaning of them is this, that when poetry becomes vocal, art must be an actual constituent. The language of art is not in the ordinary sense a mere conveyor of images;

it is the mirror of the human half of the poetical personality. As the spirit of the land can awaken the dormant senses of the watcher, so the spirit of the watcher, personified by the power of language, can conjure up cosmic thoughts. Descriptions of natural scenery can give either much less than the actual thing, or the spirit as well as the picture. And as clear are the lines when states of the mind or universal problems are being discussed. Before poetry is verbal, it is really romance. Of old romance reigned, and it is still the ideal state of elemental natures. Romance is the sensation of the mysterious and unknown to children; it is their wolf-stories, their stories of Red Indians; to others it is their folk stories; to others (and by no means as inexplicably as might be supposed) the touching loves of dukes for those very far beneath them. To others again it is the great thing it was to the romantic novelists, of which all the poets that have lived were sharers. The brain defines the wide and uncertain limits of romance, and poetry steps in with its definite demands of achievement and taste. Art is the crystallizer of the floating phantasies of romance, and the ceaseless foe of mediocrity.

These then are the two main rules we must observe if we are to define poetry ; first, to remember the extreme personality of its appeal, and secondly (which really leads out of that) to assume a certain intellectual level in the definer. The true poet is their triumphant blending. He is the artist kindled by the seer, the thinker filled with the primal feeling of romance. The spirit of poetry is a part of the universal harmony, an essence of the imagination, visible in every character, every action, every scene of the poet's creation. The poetic background may in each case be far from the conventional idea of such, but in all there flows the magic something telling of the poetic imagination. For poetry is not confined to rhymes and metres ; it penetrates through all forms of language just as its halo, the poetic imagination, interpenetrates every idea and every action. Remember that poetry is a song, and that therefore the negative qualities must be there equally with the positive. There must be no jarring notes. The true poet is a master of proportion, good taste, feeling. He rests on the firm basis of nature's sanity. He is a philosopher, not reasoning from step to step, but drinking from the fountain of ' unworded things and old '.[1] Indeed the magic of poetry is intangible atmosphere. Every poet grasps with his intense personality some fraction of the eternal beauty of the eternal things. The song of the ages is truly a song of romance. A line, a verse suddenly thrills us. It is then we hear a mystic note, faintly echoing through every fibre of our soul, from some unimagined, golden land. It is the land of El Dorado. The dreamer dreams of it, and dreaming hears the music. The poet looks out upon the stars and hears it also. The night wind softly passes by winged with murmurs, and the palpable cooling of the air is like a watch ticking off the progression of the hours. Over millions of sleepers, stars, in ageless romance and silence are beginning to rise and throw down upon them their passionate and inscrutable beams. It is strange to think of these great eyes, like the wakeful seaward gleams of lighthouses, staring for ever into dim space and looking into shoreless night, as we lie uneasily beneath them, heavily breathing in rest and weariedly sunk in oblivion. But for the poet, a song wakes from the stars and from the earth, and weaves in its melody a chain of cosmic and universal perception.

[1] *Earth and a Wedded Woman,* stanza V.

It would be a senseless and impossible plan to try to define what really mean these majestic notes, thoughts, aspirations. They are the personal relation of each individual soul to the boundless, fathomless ocean of things.

In the best sense the poet is the child of nature, that is to say he is the guardian of sanity, liberty, love.

Sanity is the true acceptance of life ; it speaks of plan and beneficence. We build on what we have, blindly grasping a sense of universal order. The meaning of life appears in proportion to the sense of sanity. Calm acceptance of inevitable events shows true knowledge of the laws of nature. Decay and regeneration unceasingly are the tide of life. Dying, we dissolve once again into the elements that are eternal. Each action, like each exertion of force, is an ever-widening eddy.

Liberty is the breaking from artificial back to natural laws. In civilization there is a constant war between the wishes of nature and the wishes of man. Nature is far-seeing, man is egoistic ; nature says, ' My laws are for the good of the race ' ; man says, ' My laws are for the good of myself '. Liberty is the passionate desire to do away with distinctions that are artificial; it is the supreme admission of the divine in man.

Sanity leads to liberty and liberty to love. For love is the aspiring evolution of the soul. It is too deep and strange a thing to summarize. It is that subtle affinity of soul to soul and wider than that, of man to aspirations, which guides us like a beacon in the night. Nature is the impersonal power of progress, love the personal.

And then again the poet is the child of Nature through knowledge of her. The happy and magnetic months are filled with a natural peace. Deliciously the spring awakes from her ghostly sleep, and summer and autumn, with all their mellowing richness, sink again to winter's slumber. And so year by year he sees clearer and clearer the unity that knits them all. True perception of the outward beauty of nature is the rare dower and noble gift of the poet. The magic of the fields and the woods is very real. A spirit seems ever to live in the picture, filling us with a sense of something there just beyond our grasp. There is always yearning at the heart of beauty, and a little sadness in the most triumphant scenes.

And let us remember that poetry is not

merely a form of expression, but is in itself a living and tremendous force. Its call is strange, personal, thrilling. If you have ever looked up at the stars and realized in a flash the tragic mystery of distance, you have heard it. If you have ever felt a thought that words would only deaden, you have heard it. For the essence of the poetical spirit is all-pervading. In many latent, in many faint, it rises through every stage of perfection. Of all matters, it is the hardest to explain, for to everyone it has some special and spiritual meaning, but faintly expressed by any combination of words. It is indeed that joy 'which passeth understanding'.

Finally, poetry is not didactic, that is to say it is not a medium for opinions. It can be made so, and with power, but that is not its primary appeal. It may be said, of course, that you cannot get away from didacticism in art, any more than from egoism in action. Well, that is a question of the inherent nobility of beauty. Ordinary teaching is something heavily laid on to the fairy surface of universal symbolism. We know well how we came to revolt from the obvious lesson, the conscious moral. Art has the elusive quality of nature, and seems to broaden and

26 GENERAL INTRODUCTION

deepen to the touch of the grasper. Merged in the fluid and ever-widening circles of nature, the poet mounts from strength to strength, flinging off from his teeming brain new and ever-changing impressions. In life there is neither rest nor finality, save the deep peace of endless, ceaseless motion, for ever and ever.

With such ideals then, should we approach the examination of poetry and the poetical imagination.

CHAPTER II

The Personality of George Meredith as explained by his Atmosphere and Style

EXEGETICAL interpretation of an author is really the comparing him with his idealized self. We admire a writer because we see in him certain things that are great, that is to say certain glimpses of those things whose meaning to us is unfathomably deep, or even those things which for some reason or other have for us a special appeal. Ordinary criticism attempts to judge an author by comparing him with others, or judging him by canons which have been formed by a consideration of the work of others, but appreciation compares him to those ideals which are our goal and his goal. If we understand an author with sympathy we seem to be able to follow his mind, and to reach forward with him to the heights which are his final aim, and which he knows he never has reached and never can reach. In other words we not only revere him for what he has done, but for what we see he tried to do. Broadly speaking, criticism is the history of literature, exegesis the appreciation of it; the former is intellect, the latter, inspiration.

Now to realise an author, to grasp just that peculiar point of view or subtle intellectual position, which may be the very salt of his work, we must understand his personality. For exegesis is far more personal than criticism. Something of the author's spirit must enter into you, before you can have that prophetic sympathy which unfolds for you his mind with a feeling of personal understanding and profound knowledge of his aims. Every great author, as I have said, touches some of those chords which are our ideals. Indeed they represent on these points our personalities amplified and explained by their own inspired vision. They mirror us on the magnified glass of their genius, and show us clearer meanings of our own thoughts. Of course it would be the absurdest thing to say that any ideal is expressed really by any word. Those who have ideals called poetry, beauty, love, romance, and so on, know perfectly well how mysterious and infinitely inexpressible such things are. No one supposes that these single words are anything but the gigantic coverings of inner worlds. A man's whole personality goes to form his ideals, and thus it is that we realize through the great personalities of others, more of those things for which we ourselves are striving. It is as important to understand the personality of an author as it is to have read his books. For this is the true mystery and the true key. It is rather strange to think that almost every writer has had the same things said about him, and that we might with a little ingenuity imagine they were all alike. The personality is the life—in fact it is the author.

And again personality shows the universal plan and idea underlying a man's work. We can in a way truly appreciate writing, and yet not fully realize it, if we lack the fundamental knowledge of the author's outlook. For this will show how everything he has written is part of him, and will open out a new sphere of criticism. We see the good and the bad, but we see that they are not wholly unconnected. Though it is possible to suppose that difference of time or mood may almost represent two distinct personalities, still the remark is certainly true as showing the link that runs through much more dissimilar work. Personality has moods and changes it is granted, but they are surely just the result of the personality and only a development of it.

There are two things by which personality is made clear to us—atmosphere and style. Atmosphere is the delicate, intangible spirit that breathes through an author's work. It is not easy to explain it, except by saying that it is the visible form of personality—visible through style which is its outward colouring. In fact atmosphere and style are those attributes which make one author Keats, and another Shelley.

Now in examining, as we are to do, the personality of George Meredith, by discovering if possible the secret of his atmosphere and the value of his style as the expression of it, we must bear in mind that, until we have done so, the other chapters of this book will not really be comprehended. For Meredith has essentially that class of mind that is either a mystery to us or perfectly understood, and between which points there is often nothing but a narrow chasm. It is that kind of mind in which we may leap from darkness to light at one bound, and that bound is his personality, which in this sense is of course his outlook.

We know very well that everyone comes before us as the representative of some certain type of mind. We sum up people and all their actions from a something in them which tinges for us everything they can possibly do. A man cannot escape from his personality any more than he can escape from himself. He is what he is, an extremely mysterious mixture and result. We can dissect him, but only so far as to show the unity of the whole, for if we cut deeper, we kill the spark of life, and behold! there lie before us those abstract words of which I have spoken, in wooden and meaningless array.

I think everyone who has studied Meredith cannot have failed to realize certain essential elements and characteristics. His very remarkable keenness of insight and philosophic perception of humanity, his deeply poetic mind touching his work as it does with a kind of universal idealization, his profound humour, and his knowledge and love of nature, are apparent to all. He is really a modern in the best sense of the word, too alert to fall into the pitfalls of the mid-Victorians, and too intellectual not to appreciate the march of progress. It is this fineness of thought that has misled many, as it causes him perhaps to pass through chains of argument in his mind's eye, and arrive at results bewildering to the onlooker. And the difficulties of his style arise on the whole from much the same cause. His intolerance of mediocrity makes him constantly alive to the charge of dulness and all its train, and to the need, not only of matter which is itself suggestive and therefore not always easy to explain, but to a form constantly invigorating, in which every sentence has been weighed and almost every word considered. This subtlety of touch is really the result of qualities that have made him see himself and be a true critic of his own writing. The frequent startling failures of great writers must always make us wonder at their amazing unselfconsciousness. You will not find in Meredith any of these abnormal lapses or constant descents into feebleness.[1] Naturally his work is not all on the same level, but there is always the feeling that he has himself under his own eye. In fact he is one of the most self-conscious of authors, and it is remarkable that those very things which

[1] Even in his obscurest poems which might be said to contradict this statement there is a profound self-consciousness at work. It is indeed an excess of compression that causes them to be so involved.

make him so, have been given him so lavishly that he has not been caught in the grosser snares of them. Seeing life deeply, he sees to the foundation of character, his own as well as any other, and grasps the absurdity of all false pretensions.

First of all, then, he is a man of intense intellectual keenness. We feel this in every sentence he writes and in the picture of every figure. We see in him the zest of mastery over complicated positions and a wakefulness perfectly calm, but perfectly prepared. He never lets proportion lose itself in a theory or existence become the slave of an idea. He is the romantic historian of life, and surely life is the most romantic of histories?

And secondly he is a poet. In my introduction to this book, I have tried to explain that the poet throws his poetical imagination into everything he writes, however far it may be from the usual poetic background. Nowhere is this more absolutely true than in the writings of George Meredith. Whatever he has written bears the mark, often strangely indescribable, of a poetic imagination. To me the names of his books and especially the names of his characters and places have that fine and peculiar felicity that springs from the brain of a poet, and we know him for one also in the masterly handling of his subject and romantic but not impossible idealization of scene and figure; truly also in his good taste and sanity—for indeed the negative qualities of the poet must be there with the positive.

Thirdly, humour is understood by Meredith, and humour in a wide sense is essential, for in a way it is the criterion of taste, and helps to prevent those mental and artistic blunders of which we have unhappy examples in even the greatest writers.

Fourthly, he knows and he loves nature. This might be called one facet of his poetical outlook, but it is so distinctly part of him and so inwound not only with his poetry but with his philosophy, that it is surely as elemental a side of his personality as is his sense of beauty. I have elsewhere in this study endeavoured to show what he means by nature, and how powerful is his double perception of her—of her beauty and of her mind. Throughout his books we are constantly being reminded by majestic and marvellous descriptions and metaphors how close she is to him, and how fully for him she rises out of that night of mysterious aloofness.

And over and above all these, though of course largely built out of them, is something else—his original grasp of his subject. Mrs. Sturge Henderson in her interesting book on Meredith lays stress on this more than once. I quote from pages 42 and 316 of her work—

'For the genius of his work lies not in its artistic perfection, nor even in its intellectual subtlety, but rather in its greatness of original outline and conception.'

'His inspiration appears to lie in his poetic grasp, the intensity of realization with which he holds to the main issue and keeps it living, in defiance of the tangles of complexity he is for ever weaving every side of it. . . .'

This indeed is an aspect of him that has struck some, not otherwise favourably impressed by his work. He has a unique perception of a problem, and even in his most fantastical creations seizes upon it with power and originality. All his books are striking and suggestive by reason of their very foundations.

It is probable that these really are the five qualities which would first and most completely strike the observation of a reader. They would not only be the first to be comprehended by him, but they would be the first and decisive ones to give him that imaginative realization of the author which sets him in a frame of inexpressible clearness. In that sudden moment or first dawn in which you grasp a great poem or a great mind, lies very often the most inspired or emotional meaning of that poem or mind. It is from this moment springs that sense of atmosphere and colour that dyes for ever all future views and studies of them. The first rapture and prophetic insight nearly always fade, and not necessarily through lack of reverence—frequently you actually understand them better afterwards and still with strong admiration—but because they cannot be again that new and unknown world they were once. In Wordsworth's *Ode to Immortality* is the tragic and eternal acknowledgment of this. And so in fixing on these obvious points, I have not merely done so because they are obvious, but because in them lies that first glimpse which is perhaps the last and truest of all. And in a way indeed they contain everything just as the words poetry or philosophy may be said to contain everything. What they certainly do contain is an essence of his personality. In his mind they have become blended, and it is this peculiar atmosphere which is the secret we are to discover.

Now it is very clear to me that we have been using these words, poetry and the others, in just that sense, which at the beginning I explained was merely the cover to the real thing. For who supposes or has much right to suppose that anyone elses uses any word in the same sense as he does, till he has had a proof of it? As a matter of fact the nuances of meaning become varied under each individual personality, and we must explain them further before they can carry much weight. For though I might be able to say, 'George Meredith is a witty writer', and the reader might be able to say, 'That is so', it does not necessarily follow that I and the reader would agree as to what was witty in his writing. In fact our fundamental standpoints on any such thing might be different, and till there is a clearing of the ground, there is a right to scepticism.

This is not the place to enter closely upon a discussion of the individual associations of the subjects we have had under inspection. In other papers in this book I have dealt with them, but here, even were it possible, it would actually be misleading to do so; for close and minute study is apt to end in a philosophic view of such subjects, and not in that kind of personal view which is to give us the atmosphere we desire. Besides this, atmosphere and personality rise from a joining of all such remarkable traits, and are not to be understood from acute observation of their individual qualities. And so we arrive at this, that to realize Meredith's outlook, it is necessary to understand not only what exactly all these features mean, but what they mean in relation to that whole, which is the junction of them all.

To approach this subject then from the point of what he has accomplished—a point which is more or less definite—rather than from that which we believe is the underlying force which has made his accomplishments such as they are, would appear the most sensible method. Let me explain this. A minute ago I stopped myself because I saw that I was drifting idly in a sea of abstract words; and we cannot well enough know how meaningless such words may be. We might say that Shakespeare and Lamb and Dickens are all humorous, but we realize very well that the humour of all three is entirely, almost fantastically, different. The extreme difficulty—a difficulty that verges on impossibility—is to explain to anyone who does not know their works very fairly well, what really humour represents to these three writers, in fact, what exactly are their personalities. I am not sure that it is even possible to explain such a thing to people who do know them, except that in this case we feel ordinary remarks will have a much finer significance. The whole thing is rather like trying to explain the exact taste of a strawberry, or the absolute meaning of music. To absorb the primary atmosphere of George Meredith you must read some, not necessarily much, of his typical work—such a novel say as *Beauchamp's Career*, such a poem as *Love in the Valley*. You must, in fact, learn from his own lips his own secrets. He alone can vivify those ideals, which others, it is true, may be able to explain; and pour into abstract words a force that makes them live not only in themselves, but in relation to their surroundings. And so it is I ask you to look really at what he did, that is at his mind which actually worked these problems, and not at what he would have done, that is at his mind untrammelled by the full glare of personal idiosyncrasy. For though our dreams are most certainly our own children, yet in these dreams we do imagine perfection along our own lines. The attempt suddenly makes us aware of our limits and, what is rather different to this, of our actual nature.

This then is the way to consider a personality like that of Meredith, though it is not the way to grasp it in that first and cosmic grasp. The critic is in the position of trying to make others understand what is to him an abstract whole, and of examining for himself the real meaning of this whole.

George Meredith has the mind of the aristocratic radical. He is an extremely cultured and refined man and never untrue to his sense of mental distinction. We see all through that real knowledge and understanding of the aristocratic horizon, which cannot be learned but is innate, and we see also that unity with freedom and with liberal ideals, which might almost have spoken to our fathers of the social revolutionary. He sympathetically understands the principles of two great classes, and so sees that in dealing with personalities it is absurd to be a bigot. It is to fight ideals and for them that he comprehends is the thing—for the maintainers and opposers of such are commonly as excellent people, and frequently much more lovable, than their most logical and bitterly logical opponents. In fact, his grip of human nature is essentially sane and unfanatical. He is the aristocrat, loving, and not superciliously, their fine and indeed their typical traits, for we feel he is one of them in spirit, and yet entirely divorced from the idea of that spirit. For instance, he is more successful in the reading of the motives and minds of his own class than of others, but what he teaches us are the problems of that universal class—which is the world.

And then the Poet. He casts over everything a certain romantic idealization, partly because he is a poet, and partly, as I have said in my introduction, because he is a creator of types, that is to say a creator of imaginative but philosophical ideals. His characters are real to what we know we have wished to find, and that is why they strike us as true and splendidly conceived. He can throw into a whole book the atmosphere of a season, or a county, or a great emotion. *Evan Harrington* has the scent of English summer, *Vittoria* the passion of Italian freedom. It is noticeable that his love-scenes and descriptions of nature are frequently made the background of each other, and are fervently imagined as glimpses of an immortal beauty. For in him there lies the great sense of universal harmony. He is not only the searcher of what we are, but of what is the type and the ideal—and in this, nature very strongly bears her part.

Through all which, do not forget that he is most human. His sympathy with different classes, his humour, have given him fairness and an understanding of actual conditions, which he uses with fulness. There is something indeed remarkable in his practical insight to motive, an insight most minute and balanced. It is not only not dulled by his idealization, but may be said to be actually strengthened by it, because dealing with types he is able to see more clearly the typical characteristics, and these laws which govern even the tiniest shades of individuality. The self-consciousness, which we spoke of before, has given him an exceedingly clear view of things, and this, added to his trained intelligence, an exceedingly clear view of the relative value of things. He has really to a noteworthy extent the power of looking at us from above and of studying the very roots of purpose ; it is in part an aspect of that comic sense on which he lays so much stress and which I have called the spirit of aloofness, that is the spirit that sees us from outside the influence of the passions that form us. To understand human nature, we must more than understand it—we must believe in improbable beliefs. This seems almost to be Meredith's position, for he is an optimist, who has exposed us with perhaps more exact penetration than any other writer.

And there are in his outlook one or two not so obvious, but entirely essential points. A study of his poetry will show a stoical and stern acceptance of life and the limits of life. Certainly, as has been pointed out by Mr Trevelyan, his philosophy is not one that is full of comfort for the weak; it is a philosophy of unselfish preparation and constant trueness to the future. His eye looks forward to the generations that are to come and to grander races, whose present guardians we ourselves are. It is a trumpet note, pellucid and clear to his followers, but to others a sound that shivers in the deadly coldness of a winter dawn.

And again, with great abstract tolerance and understanding of our faults, Meredith cannot be said to suffer fools gladly. We feel, perhaps more specially in his descriptions of women, that those he does not like he despises too much to argue about. Any falseness to nature spells worthlessness to him—though in the abstract suitable for study. It is the trend of many keen radical thinkers to be what seems strangely intolerant to certain very ordinary points of view. To Meredith such figures as Constance Asper or Lady Wathin (to take examples from only one book [1]—and might we not include Mr Warwick and Percy Dacier from the same?) are simply abhorrent—almost outside the pale. The fact is, there is one class of mind that it is hard to understand from its own satisfied standpoint, and that is the Lady Wathin type of mind of a section of the middle class. Aristocracy and democracy are both in a way poetical ideals, but that special kind of hypocritical and respectable narrow middle class is prosaic with a prosaicness that is immeasurable. Meredith has for it an antipathy of the profoundest dislike. I suppose it is more or less true that really to understand anyone you must have a certain amount of sympathy with him—if it *is* true there is one section—a small section of the great

[1] *Diana of the Crossways.*

middle-class—whom Meredith does not understand. Both this and his stern acceptance of life are very largely the result of a breaking from the sentimental positions of the earlier part of the nineteenth century; they are attempts to gauge things from a wider horizon.

But when we have said all this, it is probably his poetical conception of life which mainly defines and expounds his atmosphere. We finally come back to it, as the chief explanation. It is this in particular that has cast a glamour and a romance over his work, especially the work of his middle and greatest period. Quiet twilights deepening beneath the evening star pulse with that something which thrills through his writing. It is this also which has given him that power of idealized yet accurate local sentiment, which, as well as being the ground-work of each novel, is equally the groundwork of each figure. In idealization there is perhaps a transcending of actuality, but it is of that philosophical kind which sees things grandly equal to our wishes and beliefs. In any work of art there is a colouring that gives a tone to the whole. Meredith's works are the outcome of a mind, poetical, keen, philosophical and humorous, and these bare words come to have their glowing and living meaning beneath the spell of his individual and personal appreciation of them.

Still it is true that a wider study of George Meredith will show other elements, and there will evolve before us a more complete and a more complex figure. For at first we feel the sensation of his personality alone, but afterwards we begin to analyse to the deep foundations of his mind and outlook, and examine the intricate workings of each harmonious force. With such an aim it is perhaps desirable to take his books and divide them into those periods into which they might be said roughly to fall. For by doing so we begin to see the constant change and growth that must ever be proceeding, and thus to look to a certain extent beneath the surface of the mirror. The actual human element in a personality, apart from the god-like and mysterious, is by this method brought forward. We see a mind in process of formation or alteration and grasp the power of the things of this world upon opinions and positions however inspired. Indeed, it is what shows us, more clearly than anything else, the closeness of all greatness to ourselves.

I place his prose works into three periods—the poetry should, I think, be separately considered. The first of these consists of *Farina* and *The Shaving of Shagpat*. They are the romantic prelude to those poetical and psychological novels which form the second period. Through them runs an extravagant fancy and an intense perception of the romantic spirit of long ago. They show undoubtedly signs of a keen, perceptive intellect, but their substance is ' the green-eyed wine of old romance '.[1]

This first period is the short, exotic opening to that which includes *The Ordeal of Richard Feveral, Evan Harrington, Sandra Belloni, Vittoria, The Adventures of Harry Richmond, Beauchamp's Career—Rhoda Fleming,* by date of time included, does not seem to me on the same level of imagination or accomplishment. The characteristic of these books is a poetical idealization of background and figure joined to a keenly personal yet philosophical examination of motive and fate. They are romances and they are psychological studies. They are the product of a man so closely aware of the value of things that he has read nature from her point of view and laid bare character

[1] *Farina,* ' The White Rose Club.'

from our own internal knowledge. We must always remember that he is of all men the one who is most constantly looking at himself and for the possible snares. Thus in studying nature he has not become a sentimentalist, and in studying man he has not become a cynic. He is the sane man, filled with all the great emotions of life and art. I consider that it is in this period we observe the summit and get the truest feeling of his atmosphere. For here especially is he inspired with the spirit and essence of the scene to the exclusion of the more peculiarly personal sides of personality.

The third period starts with *The Egoist*, or possibly rather with those three short stories, *The House on the Beach, The Tale of Chloe, The Case of General Ople and Lady Camper*, and the *Essay on Comedy* (though perhaps this belongs to every period), all of which preceded it by a few years, and may be said to include every one of the later novels, *The Tragic Comedians, Diana of the Crossways, One of Our Conquerors, Lord Ormont and his Aminta, The Amazing Marriage*, though I consider the last two point to a decline which is shared indeed by *The Tragic Comedians*. This period shows a deepening of the purely psychological side of him and a less comprehensive and poetical atmosphere. Such a work as *The Egoist* is truly dramatic and powerful, but it has not the magnetic setting of *Vittoria* or *Harry Richmond*.

The poems may be said to fall more or less into all three periods—the difference in their subject and treatment is frequently that of poles—though such a reckoning is not altogether satisfactory, because they are really pioneers in spirit and epitomes of his mind, and should as such almost be classed as separate influences in any division into stages of growth or decay. Their style is not so much bounded by the date of composition as is that of the prose, which would seem to show that he could express certain thoughts through them when what was expressible in prose had entered upon a further development of his mind's age.

We have thus partially reviewed and examined certain of those traits which together form the personality and atmosphere of George Meredith—or arise from them. For indeed, I wonder how much we realize that examination of personality is perhaps only the examination of the results of personality. There is always a something which no language will explain and no philosophy account for—

that something which is the elusive spark of conscious life. Can we look into a man and follow the track of those cosmic workings which in dark and fathomless night formed themselves into the complex unity of a personality, and say to ourselves, 'Here and here were the impersonal goads to light?' It is doubtful. Rather, is it not more easy to argue that what we call the moulders of personality are partly the educators of it and partly its own natural results? In this chapter the aim, after all, is to try and represent what the feeling of Meredith's personality and atmosphere is, and this is the position from which we must here regard it. Some authors represent more than others definite and special phases of thought, and may seem therefore to be easier to explain; but I am not sure whether this is not a rather fallacious seeming, arising mainly from a clearer realization in the expounder's own brain of what he has to expound. For instance, we may say that Walt Whitman stands for the ideal of America, or Walter Pater for the ideal of renaissance culture, but till we have examined what these ideals mean we have not approached much nearer to the point. If we ask the question, What does George Meredith stand for? we shall not get so clear an answer. He stands for nothing definite in the sense that it can be defined by a concise expression, but he does stand for something definite in the sense that there is a universal plan of thought and continuity of outlook in his work. Above the attraction or repulsion which his more personal aims inspire, he does stand for a nobler and more mental comprehension of life and nature, and for a truer knowledge of the philosophical meaning of existence.

It is now necessary to say a few words about his style, in order to complete the portrait of his personality. It is not under survey from a critical standpoint, or only in so far as it emphasizes successfully or otherwise the feeling of his atmosphere. In the introduction to this book, I said how unlikely it was that style and thought would be of unequal power. They arise together from the same beginning, and are reflections of the same mind. It is inconceivable that a very witty thinker would express himself in the language of Dr Johnson. If he did so, he would simply cease to be witty to anyone but himself. In fact, style is not only the medium of thought, but is in itself a factor of imagination. How a study of poetry especially bears this in upon us. In such a statement we are certainly bounded rather closely by literature, for a thing like philosophy, which is near the borderline, requires clearness of expression first and last. There are indeed styles through which we seem to see thoughts, too great for their covering, struggling to escape, but are not these thoughts themselves generally of an unformed dimness? there are even styles which are greater than the thought behind, but it frequently means that the thought is erroneous, not false. And surely both cases only show that style is in itself an individual force. We get in Meredith's style a very good example of the oneness of thought and expression, and yet, at the same time, of the individual suggestiveness of expression. There is a fineness of touch about his style, an adaptability to the changes of his acute and eager intellect, that seem to make it almost a living thing. A friend of the poet James Thomson said to him, ' Here truly are words that if you pricked them would bleed'. The idea of this is not an exaggeration. With Meredith, language masters infinite shades. It is not only the mouthpiece but the emphasizer. It has that sureness which makes us realize positions and grasp the passing shades of change. At all times the personal side of language has been very close to him, and this has given it brilliance, self-consciousness and sometimes a sense of strain. His vocabulary is rich and suitable to any occasion. The fine selection is shown when he has to make lyrical use of language either in prose or verse, for then he rises to the needs of his subject with the perfect taste of the poet. It has been observed that in any intense or tragic moment he drops from him his sensitive and rather irritating use of words, and writes in the majestic simplicity that alone is suitable to the greatest scenes. He has made language too intellectual a medium for his style ever to be popular, and it has indeed been to some extent prejudicial to the large clearness we see in other masters. For, as I said at the beginning, he tries to make it leap at points through a string of clues. In later years a natural change has been taking place, and it has become more individualized and difficult, till the climax has been reached in his last two books, *Odes in Contribution to the Song of French History*, and *A Reading of Life*, which are both, but especially the former, extremely obscure.[1]

[1] An interesting question might be raised on the

54 PERSONALITY EXPLAINED

But on the whole his style represents quite accurately the salient features of his atmosphere. As in his personality, the chief gift of it is, in my opinion, the sense of poetry and poetic fitness—which in both is of arresting and final value. It is this surely which especially presents the intangible charm and magnetism of his atmosphere. It is this which so marks him out as an epoch-maker and so differentiates him from the writers of his own date. His mind is essentially cosmic and not local, seeing things in relation to some harmonious whole, not simply in relation to their supposed individual importance.

He is a distinguished and subtle writer, and consequently has a distinguished and subtle personality, and is not therefore to be read like an open book. But after all it is easier to understand the drift of the outlook of great men than of small men. We can, as it were, follow the working of Shakespeare's brain, but we cannot follow the working of the brain of a man who dislikes scenery. We can somehow understand the wildest flights of

artistic morality of allowing a style to be too obviously personal. An impression is abroad that Hugo is in the decline and Flaubert in the ascendant. Authoritative words on this point would command attention.

genius, but we cannot understand the motives of our next door neighbour; the first seem strangely logical, the second entirely inscrutable. For there is a universal affinity to great things, whilst to merely eccentric or small things there is only an individual affinity, which we may or may not have. We feel that George Meredith is great, and in time this feeling must become personified into a knowledge of that especial greatness which is George Meredith.

CHAPTER III

Philosophy of Nature

THESE obscure and ethereal questionings that find in nature alone a calm answer to their unrestful desires, spring from two very different types of mind. There is the type that accepts nature as she is and draws from her an ultimate gladness and philosophy, and the type that looks to her to fulfil its own yearning and ideal longings in mystic revelations of pure romance. The former see in her the sagacity of ages, and willingly realize that they themselves must be drinkers at the fountain head of her wisdom. She is to them the mother of all, and as such claims a commanding but not unthinking obedience. All nature is significant to them, and they understand her from the sane view of order and advance without losing sight of the magnetic and poetical significance of her moods and the essential mysticism of her origin and genius. They see in fact that she is the true guide to knowledge of life and is welded with themselves into a gigantic symbol of immortality. Spiritually they conceive of her as the passionless but earnest representative of truth, the relentless but benignant power of progress. They have for her a personal love and philosophic reverence that show an intimate and acute understanding of her relationship to the affairs of humanity.

And secondly, there is the class of mind that sees in nature the radiant goal of their impassioned hopes. They are searching for a super-nature, that is, a nature capable of giving emotions as gleaming and ecstatic as their own transcendent dreams. For them, seen nature is the symbol of their happy El Dorado, and the stars of midnight sing the intransient music of the spheres. They do not, like the others, bring nature into their lives, but earnestly strive to merge themselves in nature. It is in the tragic and sublime that they find an answer, and a revelation in starlight at sea or the fiery emblems of a tropical dawn. They see in nature that eternal power whose burning heart is the home of all aspiration and love and beauty. Though she is not so close to them as she is to the first class, yet she is, in herself and apart from her influence, much more personal.

There is, of course, no strict line of demarcation between these two types of mind, the thoughts of both being indeed to some extent eminently characteristic of each other, but that they are two absolute types cannot be gainsaid. To the second class belongs such a poet as Shelley, to the first class such a poet as Meredith.

I want then to examine in this chapter Meredith's perception of the romance and philosophy of nature, and in the following one his poetical ability to crystallize this perception into deep strains of music.

In attempting to define Meredith's philosophy of nature, I am aware that such ground has already been ably covered by Mr Trevelyan and others, and that what I say will not greatly, if at all, add to the truth of their conclusions. However, in that it is a difficult problem to really grasp such a writer's fine spirit, I will make an effort to lay bare my own conclusions.

To Meredith, nature signifies the inspired sanity of progress and echoes the exalted melody of eternal beauty. For him she

PHILOSOPHY OF NATURE   59

becomes close and universal, striking in him chords that show that he himself is sprung from her and is even now a unit of her all-embracing plan; and she becomes mystical and aesthetical, in the contemplation of the vast, unknown spaces and æons through which she works, and of the awful origins and aim of that giant intelligence. She is the mother, she is the goddess. We know well that we are of her, how little we know of what we are. To Meredith, this earth bounds our philosophic power of at all accurately gauging the lessons and the trends of nature. He imagines us as children of earth, sprung from its substance and endowed with meanings that are of the spirit of earth. her teaching is that of ceaseless, ordered, and perpetual advance, full of the unselfishness that comes from an obliviousness to the unrequired claims of personality, and full of the justness that arises from exact obedience to fundamental law. We must understand her from the standpoint that is founded on the senses and on the imagination. We must see that we are children, but have individualities, that we must obey, but that we must think. For we are not merely the pawns of evolution, but even movers in the great game. In us is the impersonal and the personal, both striving for the dim ideals that are perhaps in themselves no more than faith and ethical realization of advance.

For though Meredith is an optimist, it cannot be said that he is of the kind that hears the clear call of a sure hope. There is, it seems to me, a threefold optimism in the face of the unknown future. Firstly, the optimism of a faith that has become almost a certainty, in all its varieties from Browning to Shelley; secondly, the optimism that gladly and simply accepts life as in itself worth all the results of birth and death, such as Stevenson; and thirdly, the optimism that, whilst not accepting any statements of ultimate perfectibility, or perhaps not inclined to believe in the perpetuity of anything comprehensible to us as life, still with hopeful eyes seems to see the winding path of progress stretching into vistas that are ages, making existence not only good to be in, but cheerfully sacrificeable to the needs of the future. Of this class Meredith may be taken as an example. He has seen the sagacity and sureness of nature, and has learnt from her a lesson that is not altogether of the mind, but largely also of the personal susceptibility to her vivid and subtle moods. The mystic element in his philosophy of nature is strong. Indeed the rapid and varied whirlpool of the brain cannot be expected to express in other language than that of imagery one half of its amazing and radiant emotions. There are thoughts dwelling in the innermost cells of the mind that melt into nothingness before the forces of explanation and mystical notes that resound only in an unknown sensibility. It is this mysticism in Meredith that gives life and deep significance to such a poem as the noble *Hymn to Colour*. As Mr Trevelyan says (*Independent Review,* July 1904; reprinted in *The Philosophy and Poetry of George Meredith,* page 84): ' What exactly does it mean ? The answer cannot be given because to pour it into more exact words would be to spill its essence. But let us ask by way of reply : What exactly do the universe and the life of man mean ? Perhaps that knowledge cannot be put into exact words. Perhaps it is too sacred for exact words to signify it.' It is a fitting summing up of the question. In this poem lie the lyrical and harmonious rays that thread and interthread the current and basis of life. In such lines as—

62 PHILOSOPHY OF NATURE

> Love eyed his rosy memories : he sang :
> O bloom of dawn, breathed up from the gold sheaf
> Held springing beneath Orient ! [1]

or

> With Life and Death I walked when Love appeared,
> And made them on each side a shadow seem.
> Through wooded vales the land of dawn we neared,
> Where down smooth rapids whirls the helmless dream
> To fall on daylight ; and night puts away
> Her darker veil for grey.[2]

is the warmth and glowing colours of that stream which sweeps out from the well of existence. The meaning of such a poem as the *Hymn to Colour*[3] may well develop under the individuality of the reader. It is too ethereal to have any positive interpretation divorced from the personal feeling each one must have for the emotions of love, of dawn, and of romance. It may be said to represent the ideal of love wedded, as love always is, to the spirit of morning, and rising superior to night and death through its own inherent immortality. It is an effort in words

---

[1,2] *Hymn to Colour*, Stanzas ix and i.
[3] For brilliant exposition of this poem see *The Philosophy and Poetry of George Meredith*, by Mr G. M. Trevelyan, and an article in the *Independent Review* for December 1906, by Mr Basil de Selincourt.

PHILOSOPHY OF NATURE 63

to picture in colour the essence of love and dawn, an attempt to join in symbolism and imagery the arts of poetry, of painting, and of philosophy. In *Melampus* again we find this mystical comprehension of life—

> The soul of light vivid shone, a stream within stream ;
> The soul of sound from a musical shell outflew ;
> Where others hear but a hum and see but a beam,
> The tongue and eye of the fountain of life he knew.[1]

In fact, though he does not very frequently write in such directly mystical language, we can see that it is the spirit in which all his description of nature is wrought. The lyrical poet is always at heart filled with a natural mysticism, which must not of course be confounded with the superstitious mysticism of the fanatic. He is always overwhelmed with a sense of eternal things that are eternally beyond him ; he always feels a strange similitude between his highest and scarce opened thoughts and the great moments that spring from death and nature. Meredith is in a real degree the master of this sense, for he not only knows it, but has embodied it in living imagery.

[1] Stanza viii

But in this chapter we are to deal chiefly with the actual philosophy that nature, as represented by this earth, arouses in him. As I have said, he sees in her the undeviating wisdom of a beneficent but impersonal power. For though we change, nature is unchanging, and though our ideals alter, her ideals are unalterable. No cries of personal considerations are allowed to wreck the course she travels. Working in huge circles of time, she evolves for herself her true and balanced future and is ever looking forward. Perpetual progress in just and absolute sequence marks the path of her advance. Nature is not to be baulked, and if the attempt is made will simply overflow the banks until the obstacle is worn away. There is the personality of each individual life and form of life, and there is the personality of life's universal tide. We are part of nature, but in an impersonal sense that leaves play for our own individuality. It is through the awakening knowledge that we are indeed her children, that we learn to look to her, when we have far left behind us the personal influence of our relationship. There is a remarkable touch in *Richard Feverel*, where the actuality of nature's significance is suddenly aroused in

Richard's heart by the turn of his own affairs—

> The solemn gladness of his heart gave nature a tongue. Through the desolation flying overhead—the wailing of the Mother of Plenty across the bare-swept land—he caught intelligible signs of the beneficent order of the universe, from a heart newly confirmed in its grasp of the principle of human goodness, as manifested in the dear child who had just left him; confirmed in its belief in the ultimate victory of good within us, without which nature has neither music nor meaning, and is rock, stone, tree, and nothing more.[1]

It is this observation of a sane plan governing the universe, or inherent in it, that so assures Meredith. Earth cradles us, and at last, when calm night has gently shrouded this mortality of ours, resolves us once again into herself. It is from contact with her comes peace and inward rest. It is in face of the beautiful signs of her life that we gain the strength of knowledge. All over valley and woodland, and in the rain and the smell of the refreshed grass and the lights of sea and air, lie the secrets of earth's philosophy. Touch her close and vital wisdom dissipates the unhappy and complicated doubts that surround us. Earth's low murmur wakes in us the responsive note of our common origin. The agonies of diseased conscience and of

[1] Chap. x.

PHILOSOPHY OF NATURE

terror and sorrow sink away from us, and the primal feelings, that long ago woke us out of darkness, come again upon us. Better than I can explain it, will be seen Meredith's meaning in the following poem—

> Leave the uproar : at a leap
> Thou shalt strike a woodland path,
> Enter silence, not of sleep,
> Under shadows, not of wrath ;
> Breath which is the spirit's bath,
> In the old Beginnings find,
> And endow them with a mind,
> Seed for seedling, swathe for swathe.
> That gives Nature to us, this
> Give we her, and so we kiss.
>
> Fruitful is it so : but hear
> How within the shell thou art,
> Music sounds ; nor other near
> Can to such a tremor start.
> Of the waves our life is part ;
> They our running harvests bear :
> Back to them for manful air,
> Laden with the woodland's heart !
> That gives Battle to us, this
> Give we it, and good the kiss.[1]

And here again, in this next one, is another recognition of the spiritual lesson of nature—

> Sweet as Eden is the air,
> And Eden-sweet the ray.

---

[1] *Nature and Life,* stanzas i and ii (the whole poem).

PHILOSOPHY OF NATURE

> No Paradise is lost for them
> Who foot by branching root and stem
> And lightly with the woodland share
>   The change of night and day.
>
> Here all say,
> We serve her, even as I :
> We brood, we strive to sky,
> We gaze upon decay,
> We wot of life through death,
> How each feeds each we spy ;
> And is a tangle round,
> Are patient ; what is dumb,
> We question not, nor ask
> The silent to give sound,
> The hidden to unmask,
> The distant to draw near.
>
> And this the woodland saith :
> I know not hope or fear ;
> I take whate'er may come ;
> I raise my head to aspects fair,
> From foul I turn away.
>
> Sweet as Eden is the air
>   And Eden-sweet the ray.[1]

This is an interpretation of the not merely passive unselfishness that forms the elements of nature's progression. It may be a cold philosophy, but it is that which has brought us to our present state and which points forward along the road of progress.

It would be inaccurate to suppose that Meredith minimises the power of our individual personality. Nature is not entirely

[1] *Woodland Peace.*

perfect and has even inscrutable and seemingly dark methods of advance. Her scheme is perhaps too large for full understanding of it ever to be quite grasped by us. For instance, the entire lack of care for individual suffering must always appear to us too intense a disregard of the claims of the present. I do not know whether it is of this Meredith is thinking when he writes—

> He who has looked upon Earth
> Deeper than flower and fruit,
> Losing some hue of his mirth,
> As the tree striking rock at the root .. [1]

or when he says 'obedient to nature not her slave',[2] but it certainly is a point that must make us reflect. And again, nature, though simple in the sum total of her teaching, is not simple in the emotions she arouses. There is much that is incomprehensible in her, and that is to be grasped more by intuition than reason. Strange gleams spring out upon us and sink back and become nothing; sad and dim thoughts are awakened by a hundred different surroundings and majestic glimpses fade with the fading sunset. There are in

[1] *The Day of the Daughter of Hades*, section i.
[2] *The Test of Manhood*

nature just these respondent touches that make us grasp the depth and intensity of our own personality. Between us chords are quivering which can quiver for no one else. They touch in us springs of emotion and consciousness that lie in the abyss of personality; they revive in us those first echoes that are so far off and so near. As we look into nature, we see all the complicated network of her multitudinous existence and intelligence, and feel that she is working out her plan in regular and mysterious convolution. In what lies her great and elusive magnetism? Is it beauty alone that gives us that sense of atmosphere which so stamps and vivifies her different aspects, or is there really comprehensible by us a vast spirit or meaning, filling the scene and filtering through every pore of life? How often have we felt that there is something around us we are just unable to realize, an essence of something so beautiful, so melodious, that we can almost seem to hear a song wake in the bosom of the air, to open for us in a moment the secrets that hem us in upon this earth. Nature is personal to us without being directly communicative, and so elusive is she, that we must foster this understanding by efforts of imaginative communion. Only for those who study her do her clearer meanings evolve. Then only can her immemorial significance and power fully enter into us—

> The voice of nature is abroad
> This night; she fills the air with balm;
> Her mystery is o'er the land;
> And who that hears her now and yields
> His being to her yearning tones,
> And seats his soul upon her wings,
> And broadens o'er the windswept world
> With her, will gather in the flight
> More knowledge of her secret, more
> Delight in her beneficence,
> Than hours of musing, or the love
> That lives with men could ever give!
> Nor will it pass away when morn
> Shall look upon the lulling leaves,
> And woodland sunshine, Eden-sweet,
> Dreams o'er the paths of peaceful shade;
> For every elemental power
> Is kindred to our hearts, and once
> Acknowledged, wedded, once embraced,
> Once taken to the unfettered sense,
> Once claspt into the naked life,
> The union is eternal.[1]

It is then she comes to be that living example of the ancient, universal forces of the earth. In the following verse of *Earth and a Wedded Woman*, there is an extraordinarily fine rendering of this idea—

[1] *South West Wind in the Woodland.*

PHILOSOPHY OF NATURE 71

> Through night, with bedroom window wide for air,
> Lay Susan tranced to hear all heaven descend :
> And gurgling voices came of Earth, and rare,
> Past flowerful breathings, deeper than life's end
> From her heaved breast of sacred common mould ;
> Whereby this lone-laid wife was moved to feel
>   Unworded things and old
>   To her pained heart appeal.
> Rain ! O the glad refresher of the grain !
> And down in deluges of blessed rain ! [1]

Certainly for a true understanding of this revelation of a beneficent nature it is necessary to read the whole poem, for without the context the verse loses much of its real meaning.

And still look deeper than this and we see facing us the great mysteries that underlie nature and hold this earth itself in an impenetrable and silent grip. It is surely a solemn thought that we are the pawns of an absolute force and that personality can only enliven life and can by no means change the actual earthly destinies of humanity. Is it not perhaps this knowledge that has caused Meredith to lay such stress on our self-abnegation to wiser power, and learn nature's stirring lesson that victory is not necessarily the gaining of the day, but the gaining of ourselves ? In these lines, this creed is summarized—

[1] Stanza v.

The gift of penetration and embrace,
His prize from tidal battles, lost or won,
Reveals the scheme to animate his race ;
How that it is a warfare but begun ;
Unending ; with no Power to interpose ;
No prayer, save for strength to keep his ground,
Heard of the Highest ; never battle's close,
The victory complete and victor crowned :
Nor solace in defeat, save from that sense
Of strength well spent, which is the strength renewed.
In manhood must he find his competence ;
In his clear mind the spiritual food ;
God being there while he his fight maintains ;
Throughout his mind the Master Mind being there,
While he rejects the suicide despair,
Accepts the spur of inexplicable pains ;
Obedient to Nature, not her slave :
Her lord, if to her rigid laws he bows ;
Her dust, if with his conscience he plays knave,
And bids the Passions on the Pleasures browse . .[1]

Then too there is a certain sternness in nature. Her freedom from sentimentality, on which we most of us lean as an excuse and as a comfort, gives us at first an uneasy feeling that all is not perfectly well with us. It is the dawn of our new searching of ourselves. The still and relentless questions of nature cannot be shunned, her even, eternal sentences cannot be avoided. It is better then that we should consciously face the ordeal with all the equipment a keen and eager intelligence

[1] *The Test of Manhood.*

PHILOSOPHY OF NATURE 73

suggests. Nature means still more to Meredith than simply the emotional stimulus of her outward loveliness. She dwells not only in the scene but in ourselves, not only in the woods but in the streets. She is around everything and in everything. The intangible and rare spirit is made visible through a use of the experiences of both town and country. For we are under the spell of her laws just as much as is inanimate nature. Meredith says in *Earth's Secret*—

> Not solitarily in fields we find
> Earth's secret open, though one page is there;
> Her plainest, such as children spell, and share
> With bird and beast; raised letters for the blind.
> Not where the troubled passions toss the mind,
> In turbid cities, can the key be bare.
> It hangs for those who hither thither fare,
> Close interthreading nature with our kind.
> They, hearing History speak, of what men were,
> And have become, are wise. The gain is great
> In vision and solidity; it lives.
> Yet at a thought of life apart from her,
> Solidity and vision lose their state,
> For Earth, that gives the milk, the spirit gives.

Nature's influence over us comes in fact through very different channels; through that of the outward observation as well as through that of the inward sympathy. Firstly we are her children and bound by the laws of which we are the result; secondly, we are units of nature, inherently swayed by her and capable of innate mental influence to the nobility of beauty, but at the same time, as the result of this semi-individuality, owning a relative direction over the development of these powers; and thirdly, we are watchers of nature, gathering a philosophy from the lessons of her passing life. In a word, it might be said we are firstly, unconsciously, nature; secondly, consciously, children of nature; thirdly, observers of nature. I think it is not altogether fanciful to suppose that Meredith has comprehended all these attitudes to nature, though, as it is not necessary to say, they work into one another, till one sentence may hold the essence of them all. For instance, in the beautiful *Dirge in Woods*, the whole spiritual essence of the poem is carried by a simile into a philosophical comparison between man's mortality and life's immortality—

> A wind sways the pines,
>   And below
> Not a breath of wild air;
> Still as the mosses that glow
> On the flooring and over the lines
> Of the roots here and there.
> The pine-tree drops its dead,
>   They are quiet, as under the sea.
> Overhead, overhead
> Rushes life in a race,
> As the clouds the clouds chase;
>   And we go,

PHILOSOPHY OF NATURE

And we drop like the fruits of the tree,
Even we,
Even so.

And in such a way Meredith constantly uses nature to point the metaphor at man. For in a universally obvious sense, she holds certain attributes needful to the cause of our forward step. In her sacrifice of the individual to the type, in her unhasting and perpetual laws, in her providence and far-sightedness, there are the wide signs of a self-sacrifice, a sanity, a wisdom, that are the salt of our ethical philosophy. And, in a sense perhaps unexplainable, the physical aspect to nature brings us back to the simple and primal things of life. To Richard Feverel, in the storm in the Rhineland forest,[1] comes suddenly, as if scales had fallen from his eyes, a just appreciation of his position; to Sandra Belloni, sitting by Wilming Weir in the moonlight,[2] a calm peace in knowledge of the fulness of love; to Dr Shrapnel, walking in his garden at sunset,[3] a strengthening and renewal of all his ideals; to Beauchamp and Renée, spellbound before the glory of a Venetian sunrise,[4] the thrill of inspired passion;

[1] *The Ordeal of Richard Feverel*, chap. xlii.
[2] *Sandra Belloni*, chap. xx.
[3] *Beauchamp's Career*, chap. xii.
[4] *Beauchamp's Career*, chap. ix.

to Matey Weyburn and Aminta, in their seaward morning swim,[1] an understanding of what they mean to one another. I need not continue the list. It is a sign that clearly shows the working of this mysterious influence —an influence both physical and mental. We are simplified and purified by contact with the reality of nature. There is about her something so actual, true, beautiful, that before her there drops from us the artificial structure of our acute civilization. Once more we face her, as long ago man faced the sun filled strangely with inexpressible thoughts.

In considering such things as the wisdom and sanity of nature we must of course be aware lest we read into her the very moods that arise in our own minds from observation of her changing phases. We cannot really suppose that she passes through all those stages of joy and sadness which we so vividly imagine. On a November afternoon, when evening is beginning to settle over the silent earth, and a mist is creeping along the valley, wreathing in dim and mysterious folds every tree and outline and noiselessly enveloping the landscape in still thicker darkness, we do seem to feel around

[1] *Lord Ormont and his Aminta*, chap. xxvii.

us a strange and sad spirit breathing its cold breath upon the earth beneath. And as the night closes in and the stillness seems to deepen beneath the glittering moon, surely there falls upon us a feeling as of eternal slumber and a sense as of the night of all things. It is not so much death that we feel near us as a sleep that is life in death. And yet is not all this imagery the result of the external appearance of the scene working on our active but localized intelligences? Under it all, nature is pursuing her calm and unchequered course. For this sanity of hers is a fundamental lesson in her philosophy. Meredith never tires of impressing this upon us. Year in and year out she works forward upon the gigantic circles of her progression. Do we really suppose that a June night, crowned with song and the smell of roses, holds something in it more majestic than all the other nights of the year! Far in the breast of nature, her heart is beating in ever even throbs, and her secrets are always open to the earnest seeker—

> Verily now is our season of seed,
> Now in our Autumn; and Earth discerns
> Them that have served her in them that can read.
> Glassing, where under the surface she burns,

78 PHILOSOPHY OF NATURE

> Quick at her wheel, while the fuel, decay,
> Brightens the fire of renewal: and we?
> Death is the word of a bovine day,
> Know you the breast of the springing To-be.[1]

Such sanity is one of the signs of the elemental and cosmic laws. It is, as it were, a realization for us of the everlasting meaning of power and order. In Meredith's sonnet, *Lucifer in Starlight*, we see an embodiment of this idea—

> On a starred night Prince Lucifer uprose.
> Tired of his dark dominion swung the fiend
> Above the rolling ball in cloud part screened,
> Where sinners hugged their spectre of repose.
> Poor prey to his hot fit of pride were those.
> And now upon his western wing he leaned,
> Now his huge bulk o'er Afric's sands careened,
> Now the black planet shadowed Arctic snows.
> Soaring through wider zones that pricked his scars
> With memory of the old revolt from Awe,
> He reached a middle height, and at the stars,
> Which are the brain of heaven, he looked, and sank
> Around the ancient track marched rank on rank.
> The army of unalterable law.

There is in this poem a peculiarly thrilling conception of a daring thought, and the atmosphere of space and finality is grandly imagined in that theatre of the sky.

We must remember that nature in us calls out also for the fulfilment of her law of sanity.

[1] *Seed-time*, stanza vi.

PHILOSOPHY OF NATURE

We too are the outcome of her mind, and cannot with safety overstrain the uses she has laid upon brain and body—

> Pleasures that through blood run sane
> Quickening spirit from the brain
> Each of each in sequent birth,
> Blood and brain and spirit, three
> (Say the deepest gnomes of Earth),
> Join for true felicity.
> Are they parted, then expect
> Some one sailing will be wrecked. .[1]

The unselfishness of nature is as remarkable as her sanity, and indeed is only one method of reaching the high aim of her wisdom. Earnestly striving to a more perfect expression of herself, she recks not of present pain and death in the certainty of ultimate improval. The type advances, the individual sinks dead. Study earth, says Meredith, and this incomprehensible thing will assume a clearer complexion. The love that springs from knowledge will unfold secrets now darkly hidden in silence—

> Love born of knowledge, love that gains
> Vitality as Earth it mates,
> The meaning of the Pleasures, Pains,
> The Life, the Death, illuminates.

---

[1] *The Woods of Westermain,* section iv.

> For love we earth, then serve we all;
> Her mystic secret then is ours:
> We fall, or view our treasures fall,
> Unclouded, as beholds her flowers
>
> Earth, from a night of frosty wreck,
> Enrobed in morning's mounted fire,
> When lowly, with a broken neck,
> The crocus lays her cheek to mire.[1]

And finally, nature's philosophy is of deepest meaning to us when life has least to offer. In the hopeless minutes of death, in the profound gloom that surrounds us like utter night and fills us with a terrible despair, there is still heard a solemn voice offering us the impressive and perpetual truths of life—

> Accept, she says; it is not hard
> In woods; but she in towns
> Repeats, accept; and have we wept,
> And have we quailed with fears,
> Or shrunk with horrors, sure reward
> We have whom knowledge crowns;
> Who see in mould the rose unfold,
> The soul through blood and tears.[2]

In these calm, even sentences is the final word of her teaching, and the last triumph of her philosophy.

[1] *The Thrush in February*, last three stanzas.
[2] *Outer and Inner*, stanza v.

CHAPTER IV

Lyrical View of Nature

I SAID in the beginning of the last chapter that I should continue in this the study of Meredith's relationship to nature. We examined then his philosophy of nature, and here I wish to examine his sense of her beauty. I have tried to show that even on the philosophic side it is a lyrical relationship, that is to say, that even whilst endeavouring to find subtle meanings and philosophies underlying the metaphors and descriptions of nature, it is yet a deeply poetical emotion, carried out in similarly poetical phraseology, that has induced him to seek such comparisons and examples. And so, though we are to put off from ourselves here all sense of the direct teacher, and simply judge of him as a poet and as a weaver of webs of colour, we must fundamentally realize as part of our emotions the nobility and essential philosophy of his descriptions. It would be perhaps unnecessary to say this, did I not wish to show the logical relationship that does exist between the different aspects through which, in his writings, nature may be viewed, and more especially to point out the great splendour and durability that surrounds all supremely beautiful descriptions. For it seems to me that those passages in which, let us say, a sunset remains for ever fixed in a burning and wonderful sleep, contain something more lasting than those which teach, with perhaps startling and realistic veracity, the selfishness of our race, or the certainty of death. Something there is in a sunset far more eternal than the ethics of many philosophers, far more assuring than the faiths of many teachers. And thus, in dealing with nature, I think the poet is great in proportion as he arouses these nameless and beautiful dreams.

We shall never understand Meredith's relationship to nature till we clearly realize his intense love for her as the outward symbol of beauty and life. In his earlier work especially there is a delight in the open air, a sense of atmosphere, to equal which we must go to the descriptions of Walt Whitman or Turgenieff. Whether it be the seasons, or the hours of day from sunrise to moonlight, he gives in his language the feeling and the distinct personality of the moment, imaging with intense and glowing fervour the salient, which are indeed the poetic and romantic, features of the scene. There is in him too most strongly the joy of living, the joy, that is to say, of swiftly walking across springy grass, of climbing mountains, of breathing, existing, being alive on the earth. I do not know whether I shall be considered rash in asserting that it is in these sentences in which he pictures for us the spirit and aspect of nature that he rises to the summit of his powers. It is in such sentences that we most feel the sense and assertion of genius, and recognize a poetic sway of language which is truly great. Here he throws off from him the direct cult of didacticism, which I cannot help thinking lessens the real meaning of poetry. Here he becomes supremely conscious of the unique majesty and romance of the stars above, and the earth beneath. How beautiful for example are his descriptions of the morning—

Happy happy time, when the white star hovers
   Low over dim fields fresh with bloomy dew,
Near the face of dawn, that draws athwart the darkness,
   Threading it with colour, like yewberries the yew.
Thicker crowd the shades as the grave East deepens
   Glowing, and with crimson a long cloud swells.

Maiden still the morn is ; and strange she is, and secret ;
Strange her eyes ; her cheeks are cold as cold seashells.[1]

The phrase, 'When the white star hovers low over dim fields fresh with bloomy dew', always pictures to me those rich, low-lying meadows that stretch on either side a river just beginning to glitter beneath the morning star. In *Diana of the Crossways*, he says that a poor writer can describe the sunset, but that it needs a poet ' to sing the dawn '.[2] And this is his song, and how true. For when the east is on the point of awaking, there is in the air that feeling of strangeness and secrecy of which he here speaks the word. Now has the first touch of morning kindled the sky. It is not indeed the true dawn, but the herald of it. There are no startling contrasts, as of crimson, raying across the blackness of night's curtain, or of golden-edged clouds floating like fireships through the air. All this will come some short hour hence. But now there is nothing but a strange, ethereal light, suffused with faintest pink and saffron, and expanding so gradually and evenly, that its growth is hard to follow. A chill breath passes. Not yet

[1] *Love in the Valley*, stanza vii.
[2] Chap. xvi.

LYRICAL VIEW OF NATURE 85

has sleep fled into the mist. All is still. It is the hour before the dawn.

And again—

A night of May leaning on June, is little more than a deliberate wink of the eye of light. Mr. Barmby, an exile from the ladies by reason of an addiction to tobacco, quitted the forepart of the vessel at the first greying. Now was the cloak of night worn threadbare, and grey astir for the heralding of gold, day visibly ready to show its warmer throbs. The gentle waves were just a stronger grey than the sky, perforce of an interfusion that shifted gradations ; they were silken, in places oily grey ; cold to drive the sight across their playful monotonousness for refuge on any far fisher-sail.[1]

which is indeed a delicious picture of a spring sunrise upon the English Channel. Here again is the spirit of morning—

Morning swam on the lake in her beautiful nakedness, a wedding of white and blue, of purest white and bluest blue. Alvan crossed the island bridges when the sun had sprung on his shivering fair prey, to make the young fresh Morning rosy, and was glittering along the smooth lake-waters.[2]

and here is a description of dawn in the Alps as seen from the Adriatic—

He was awakened by light on his eyelids, and starting up beheld the many pinnacles of grey and red rocks and shadowy high white regions at the head of the gulf waiting for the sun ; and the sun struck them. One by

---

[1] *One of our Conquerors*, chap. xiv.
[2] *The Tragic Comedians*, chap. xv.

one they came out in crimson flame, till the vivid host appeared to have stepped forward. The shadows on the snow-fields deepened to purple below an irradiation of rose and pink and dazzling silver. There of all the world you might imagine Gods to sit. A crowd of mountains endless in range, erect, or flowing, shattered and arid, or leaning in smooth lustre, hangs over the gulf. The mountains are sovereign Alps, and the sea is beneath them. The whole gigantic body keeps the sea, as with a hand, to right and left.[1]

But it is especially in his drawing of twilight and moonlight that he is unique. He seems to catch for us the fleeting essence of the evening song of earth, and fix for ever the evanescent emotions of night. He has grasped as few others have done the spiritual individuality and deep mysticism of such moments. It is as if he had heard all of a sudden the imaginary melody of the spheres of which happy dreamers have told us, and had seen that earth and all that rises round us in deep and silent significance was joining too in that eternal harmony. His language shows to us the spirit of earth, a spirit full of a voice, and a meaning just beyond the powers of our comprehension. In this song, written in very early youth, there is already the mastery of this art—

---

[1] *Beauchamp's Career*, chap. ix.

LYRICAL VIEW OF NATURE 87

Oh joy thus to revel all day, till the twilight turns us homeward !
Till all the lingering deep-blooming splendour of sunset is over,
And the one star shines mildly in mellowing hues, like a spirit
Sent to assure us that light never dieth, though day is now buried.

Saying ; to-morrow, to-morrow, few hours intervening ; that interval
Turned by the woodlark in heaven, to-morrow my semblance, far eastward
Heralds the day 'tis my mission eternal, to seal and to prophecy.

Come then, and homeward : passing down the close path of the meadows,
Home like the bees stored with sweetness ; each with a lark in the bosom,
Trilling for ever, and oh ! will yon lark ever cease to sing up there ? [1]

and again in this extract, dating from about the same time—

Deeper the stillness hangs on every motion ;
Calmer the silence follows every call :
Now all is quiet save the roosting pheasant,
The bell-wether tinkle and the watch dog's bark.
Softly shine the lights from the silent kindling homestead,
Stars of the hearth to the shepherd in the fold . .[2]

There is in these simple, unrhymed lyrics the actual emotion of summer twilight. Of a much later date is the following verse—

[1] *Pastoral vii.*   [2] *Pastoral v.*

> Lovely are the curves of the white owl sweeping
>   Wavy in the dusk—lit by one large star.
> Lone on the fir-branch, his rattle-note unvaried,
>   Brooding o'er the gloom, spins the brown evejar.
> Darker grows the valley, more and more forgetting . . .[1]

I think the last line is one that shows almost more than any other his extraordinary power of observation, mixed with the true poetic feeling. When the yellow sky of a summer evening has grown into a dead grey and from that to a transparent blackness, there is still one more stage to be accomplished before the night settles into its sleep. Presently a white opaque mist will begin to rise from the ground and, slowly spreading through the darkness, will at last blot out every outline and reflection. The whole valley will seem literally to be one personality sinking into profound rest, one vast spirit gliding into forgetfulness and spinning like a planet through oblivion with the low hum of infinite motion. 'Darker grows the valley, more and more forgetting.'

The tenderness of twilight is felt by him and the peace of the mellow hour that lulls the senses—

> Mother of the dews, dark eyelashed twilight,
> Low-lidded twilight, o'er the valley's brim [2]

---

[1] *Love in the Valley*, stanza v.
[2] *Love in the Valley*, stanza x.

LYRICAL VIEW OF NATURE

The hues of sunset had left the West. No light was there but the steadfast pale eye of twilight.[1]

The direct sensations aroused by the time are probably much the same in all poetically-minded people. The brain begins to yield to thoughts completely harmonious to its surroundings. Rest and calm are in the air, and night is duskily preparing the path of sleep. Things take on a fantastic appearance of unreality as if aerially hung in a rosy haze. Meredith in *Modern Love* uses the expression, ' the largeness of the evening earth ',[2] and it is graphically reminiscent of such feelings of strangeness, when with the reddened sky, and the sun melting into blue hills, the world looms huge and unearthly around us, and dreams, not less beautiful than transient, pass us onward to the realm of night—

> I turned and looked on heaven awhile, where now
> The moor-faced sunset broaden'd with red light;
>   Threw high aloft a golden bough,
>   And seemed the desert of the night
> Far down with mellow orchards to endow.[3]

And soon through the deepening twilight will rise the summer stars and the summer

[1] *The Ordeal of Richard Feverel*, chap. xxii.
[2] Stanza xlvii.
[3] *The Orchard and The Heath*, stanza xi.

moon. The stars are like jewels set in the velvet softness of that sky, and the moon mounts upwards on a track of fire. Meredith's descriptions of moments like these are the real essence of the romance of atmosphere. They really do hold in them the breathless splendour of such times, the perpetual and universal nobility of such sensations. I think I am right in quoting freely for the purpose of justifying such strong expressions of certitude. I give first some words on the moon—

The rounded ball of the brilliant September moon hung still aloft, lighting a fathomless sky as well as the fair earth.[1]

After the early evening dinner, when sunlight and the colours of the sun were beyond the western mountains, they pushed out on the lake. A moon was overhead, seeming to drop lower on them as she filled with light.[2]

Emilia leaned to him more, and the pair fixed their eyes on the moon, that had now topped the cedar, and was pure silver; silver on the grass, on the leafage, on the waters. And in the West, facing it, was an arch of twilight and tremulous rose; as if a spirit hung there over the shrouded sun.[3]

. . . while the moon slipped over banks of marble into fields of blue, and all the midnight promised silence.[4]

---

[1] *Vittoria,* chap. ix.
[2] *Vittoria,* chap. xxxviii.
[3] *Sandra Belloni,* chap. xx.
[4] *Sandra Belloni,* chap. xii.

LYRICAL VIEW OF NATURE

She pointed to a place beside herself on the fork of a dry log under flowering hawthorn. A pale shadowy blue centre of light among the clouds told where the moon was. Rain had ceased, and the refreshed earth smelt all of flowers, as if each breeze going by held a nosegay to their nostrils.[1]

The waters streamed on endlessly into the golden arms awaiting them. The low moon burnt through the foliage. In the distance, over a reach of the flood, one tall aspen shook against the lighted sky.[2]

I do not think it is possible to question the essential poetry of these descriptions. The first two especially, with the idea of the moon hanging in 'a fathomless sky', and of the moon 'seeming to drop lower on them as she filled with light', are very beautiful. They are compact of that still and immortal passion of the night. There is perhaps little to be gained by a free use of ecstatic adjectives in describing all things like this, but the mastery of these words is of the highest order. They place you on the spot and breathe into you the actual spirit of the scene. You will remember the first finding of Sandra Belloni by the family of the Poles when in the evening woods they hear a voice singing an Italian air and 'a sleepy fire of early

[1] *Sandra Belloni*, chap. xii.
[2] *Evan Harrington*, chap. xxiii.

moonlight, hung through the dusky fir branches'.[1] Does it not summon up vividly the feeling of the time and hour? Praise could not well be greater.

And of the stars also he has written in such serene and undimmed words—

A sharp breath of air had passed along the dews, and all the young green of the fresh season shone in white jewels. The sky, set with very dim distant stars, was in grey light round a small brilliant moon. Every space of earth lifted clear to her; the woodland listened; and in the bright silence the nightingales sang loud.[2]

Bright Sirius! that when Orion pales
To dotlings under moonlight still art keen . .[3]

They set their eyes towards the dark gulf ahead. The night was growing starry. The softly ruffled Adriatic tossed no foam.[4]

The boat leaving Venice behind and pressing forward into the darkness whilst the night grows alive with stars above and the gentle breeze laps the water round it, is a picture, indelible and perfect.

Here, too, are some magnificently thoughtful lines. Perhaps they bring us as near to the true spirit of the star-gazer as can well be imagined—

---

[1] *Sandra Belloni*, chap. ii.
[2] *Sandra Belloni*, chap. lviii.
[3] *The Star Sirius*.
[4] *Beauchamp's Career*, chap. viii.

> What links are ours with orbs that are
>   So resolutely far:
> The solitary asks, and they
> Give radiance as from a shield:
>   Still at the death of day,
>   The seen, the unrevealed
>   Implacable they shine
> To us who would of Life obtain
> An answer for the life we strain,
>   To nourish with one sign.[1]

There comes a moment when detachment from the earth becomes almost a reality in looking up at the stars and merging ourselves in thoughts of their ordered motions, and in speculations on the mathematical certainty of their journeys. Dante is said to have profounder imagination than Milton, because he defined his heaven and hell accurately in his brain, whereas Milton allowed his impression to be one of vague immensity; and, in a similar way, some knowledge of the sky seems to enlarge the imaginative grasp of its romance and of its fiery and eternal stars.

Evening and early moonlight are the hours of widest communion with certain phases of the unplumbed desires of our souls. I do not know whether it be the sentiment of darkness and starlight that brings forth these inherent

---

[1] *Meditation under Stars.*

longings, but so it is. Something there would appear to be in us in rapport with the mystery of night. For the thoughts which we know in ourselves to be great and divine appear then palpably to expand and become suffused. We seem drawn into the vortex of an everlasting romance and aspiration, and our emotions react and are reacted on by what is about us. I suppose that this sentiment of romance that summer nights contain must colour all similar latent ideas in ourselves and give to cosmic imaginings a real significance. Meredith frequently places his most passionate love-scenes in such surroundings of night or twilight as give us at once the atmosphere of the picture. Here is the kind of example I mean—

> A half-circle of high-banked greensward, studded with old park-trees, hung round the roar of the water; distant enough from the white-twisting fall to be mirrored on a smooth heaved surface, while its outpushing brushwood below drooped under burdens of drowned reed flags that caught the foam. Keen scent of hay, crossing the dark air, met Emilia as she entered the river-meadow. A little more, and she saw the white weir-piles shining, and the grey roller just beginning to glisten to the moon. Eastward on her left, behind a cedar, the moon had cast off a thick cloud, and shone through the cedar-bars with a yellowish hazy softness, making rosy gold of the first passion of the tide, which, writhing and straining on through many lights, grew

LYRICAL VIEW OF NATURE

wide upon the wonderful velvet darkness underlying the wooded banks. With the full force of a young soul that leaps from beauty seen to unimagined beauty, Emilia stood and watched the picture. Then she sat down, hushed, awaiting her lover.[1]

In the bosom of night, the scents and sounds of day become blended into one slumbrous murmur. There is an effect in the air that precludes discord and works all things into a subtle undertone of melody. How gently beats the vast heart of night. A quiet breathing is around us, and steeps us in its spirit. I quote two verses as illustrative of this mood, and they are amongst the most lyrical and rhythmical that he has written—

> The soft night wind went laden to death
> With smell of the orange in flower;
> The light leaves prattled to neighbour ears;
> The bird of the passion sang over his tears;
> The night named hour by hour.
>
> Sang loud, sang low the rapturous bird
> Till the yellow hour was nigh,
> Behind the folds of a darker cloud:
> He chuckled, he sobbed, alow, aloud;
> The voice between earth and sky.[2]

It is not necessary to give any more instances of Meredith's feeling for the night, and power of rendering it. His own words

[1] *Sandra Belloni*, chap. xx.
[2] *The Young Princess*, section iv, stanzas i and ii.

are expressive of this, and give that sense of sympathy which it is apparent must exist between ourselves and those things which we seek to describe. As he says—

> . . . I, who love old hymning night
> And know the Dryad voices well . .[1]

And just as there is a personality interweaving the surface of morning and night, so clearly is it with all the other aspects of nature. The seasons are embodiments of the flow or sleep of an inward current. The poet of spring or summer or autumn or winter must have for his first asset a knowledge of their real relationship to definite ideals. He must see that there is everywhere a life which can only be realized for others by an intense knowledge in ourselves of its actual individuality. In such an expression as ' It was a magnificent evening ' there is no atmosphere, that is to say, there is no rendering of the spirit of evening. The typical beauty of nature can only be given by thoughts and language equally beautiful and suggestive. Meredith being a poet, has seen nature through the eyes of the poet and has described her in the language of the poet. Thus spring

[1] *Ode to the Spirit of Earth in Autumn.*

holds for him a voice that is the song of morning—

> Out in the yellow meadows, where the bee
> Hums by us with the honey of the Spring,
> And showers of sweet notes, from the larks on wing,
> Are dropping like a noon-dew, wander we.[1]

and—

The day was a van-bird of summer: the robin still
    piped, but the blue,
A warm and dreamy palace with voices of larks ringing
    through
Look'd down as if wistfully eyeing the blossoms that fell
    from its lap:
A day to sweeten the juices, a day to quicken the sap!
All round the shadowy orchard sloped meadows in gold,
    and the dear
Shy violets breathed their hearts out: the maiden
    breath of the year![2]

And summer, a voice that is the song of life—

> Busy in the grass the early sun of summer
> Swarms, and the blackbird's mellow fluting notes
> Call my darling up with round and roguish challenge:
> Quaintest, richest carol of all the singing throats![3]

And then as summer wanes towards autumn a new note is heard, the note of heat, lassitude, and the sultry warmth of continued sunshine—

Doves of the fir-wood walling high our red roof
    Through the long noon coo, crooning through the coo.

---

[1] *Modern Love*, stanza xi.
[2] *Grandfather Bridgeman*.
[3] *Love in the Valley*, stanza xvii.

Loose droop the leaves, and down the sleepy roadway
  Sometimes pipes a chaffinch ; loose droops the blue.
Cows flap a slow tail, knee-deep in the river,
  Breathless, given up to sun and gnat and fly.[1]

Each season is the bearer of a thousand messages, that spring into being with the passing days, and rise into life upon the decay of others. Every new day speaks of change, every new week shows visible signs of it. Summer that started with the low hum of universal growth, closes with the low hum of universal harvest. The mellow hours ripen the raw seed to fruition, and death has in it the germs of all existence. The spirit of harvest is finely pictured by Meredith—

Yellow with birdfoot-trefoil are the grass-glades ;
  Yellow with cinquefoil of the dew-grey leaf ;
Yellow with stonecrop ; the moss-mounds are yellow ;
  Blue-necked the wheat sways, yellowing to the sheaf.
Green-yellow bursts from the copse the laughing yaffle ;
  Sharp as a sickle is the edge of shade and shine :
Earth in her heart laughs looking at the heavens,
  Thinking of the harvest : I look and think of mine.[2]

It is a description like this that makes us see the essential qualities of such a time. In face of it, we really do feel its individuality and significance and poetry. The aim of

[1] *Love in the Valley*, stanza xix.
[2] *Love in the Valley*, stanza xv.

LYRICAL VIEW OF NATURE

the poetical writer on nature is to grasp the ideal, and make us comprehend through that the actual picture.

And when autumn has yielded to winter, there is still around us an intimate sense of an actuality. The air contains a something that is the living breath of winter. Everything is gliding into unconsciousness and dimly sinking into rest. Nature's comatose sleep is falling over the earth, and soon night itself will not keep deeper silence than the forces of outward life. Once again has Meredith seized the meaning and essence of such signs—

> Those winter mornings are divine. They move so noiselessly. The earth is still, as if waiting. A wren warbles, and flits through the lank drenched brambles; hillside opens green; elsewhere is mist, everywhere expectancy. They bear the veiled sun like a sangreal aloft to the wavy marble flooring of stainless cloud.[1]

And the last scene of all this pageant of the seasons is the trance of very winter. Death seems to be the crown of life, and snow and cold the signs of its victory. Things shiver in a horrible grip of destruction, and everywhere are strewn the wrecks of life. Such are real winter nights when the light of the

[1] *The Adventures of Harry Richmond,* Chap. xxxiii.

frosty moon strikes a keen and metallic radiance upon the earth and the stars shine gleamingly above with a preternatural clearness. The brilliant air brings the heavens close. The sky so studded with circling points of fire hangs over us, as if to show the destiny of things wheeling onwards in its lonely and eternal silence. Strange indeed are the thoughts which the winter sky rouses in us. At no period does fate appear more impersonal, resistless, passionless. There is certainly an awful passion of the stars, but it is so inhuman and so far beyond us that it only tends to emphasise our own isolation. And round us earth itself seems to echo this desolation. It is like the region of lasting ice, where no life can exist but only universal night and oblivion.

Meredith has caught the feeling of such a winter night—

> Out in the freezing darkness the lambs bleat.
> The small bird stiffens in the low starlight.[1]

There is too a special glamour attached to all the different types and manifestations of nature. Mountains, water, clouds, woods, have a poetical significance, peculiar and

---

[1] *Modern Love*, stanza xxiii.

LYRICAL VIEW OF NATURE

inspiring. Here are two descriptions of mountains, which are drawn from the rarified air of the heights—

Walking was now high enjoyment, notwithstanding the force of the sun, for they were a hardy couple, requiring no more than sufficient nourishment to combat the elements with an exulting blood. Besides they loved mountain air and scenery, and each step to the ridge of the pass they climbed was an advance in splendour. Peaks of ashen hue and pale dry red and pale sulphur pushed up, straight, forked, twisted, naked, striking their minds with an indeterminate ghostliness of Indian, so strange they were in shape and colouring. These sharp points were the first to greet them between the blue and green. A depression of the pass to the left gave sight of the points of black fir forest below, round the girths of the barren shafts. Mountain blocks appeared, pushing up in front, and a mountain wall and woods on it, and mountains in the distance, and cliffs riven with falls of water that were silver skeins, down lower to the meadows, villages and spires, and lower finally to the whole valley of the foaming river, field and river seeming in imagination rolled out from the hand of the heading mountain.[1]

Poetic rhapsodists in the vales below may tell you of the joy and grandeur of the upper regions, they cannot pluck you the medical herb. He gets that for himself who wanders the marshy ledge at nightfall to behold the distant Sennhuttchen twinkle, who leaps the green-eyed crevasses, and in the solitude of an emerald alp stretches a salt hand to the mountain kine.[2]

And the following sentence is the realization of the mountains' night—

[1] *The Amazing Marriage,* chap. v.
[2] *The Adventures of Harry Richmond,* chap. liii

LYRICAL VIEW OF NATURE

Thus it happened, that seven years after his bereavement, Lord Ormont and Philippa and Bobby were on the famous Bernese Terrace, grandest of terrestrial theatres where soul of man has fronting him earth's utmost majesty.[1]

For a description of a forest gasping heavily in the heat just before a summer-storm, this is remarkable—

> An oppressive slumber hung about the forest branches. In the dells and on the heights was the same dead-heat. Here where the brook tinkled it was no cool-lipped sound, but metallic, and without the spirit of water. Yonder in a space of moonlight on lush grass, the beams were as white fire to sight and feeling. No haze spread around. The valleys were clear, defined to the shadows of their verges, the distances sharply distinct, and with the colours of day but slightly softened. Richard beheld a roe moving across a slope of sward far out of rifle-mark. The breathless silence was significant, yet the moon shone in a broad blue heaven. Tongue out of mouth trotted the little dog after him; couched panting when he stopped an instant; rose weariedly when he started afresh. Now and then a large white night-moth flitted through the dusk of the forest.[2]

And for a description of a wood at night-time in early May, this is adequate—

> With splendour of a silver day,
> A frosted night had opened May:
> And on that plumed and armoured night,
> As one close temple hove our wood,
> Its border leafage virgin white.
> Remote down air an owl hallooed.

---

[1] *Lord Ormont and His Aminta*, chap. xxx.
[2] *The Ordeal of Richard Feverel*, chap. xlii.

LYRICAL VIEW OF NATURE 103

> The black twig dropped without a twirl;
> The bud in jewelled grasp was nipped;
> The brown leaf cracked a scorching curl;
> A crystal off the green leaf slipped.
> Across the tracks of rimy tan,
> Some busy thread at whiles would shoot;
> A limping minnow-rillet ran,
> To hang upon an icy foot.[1]

There is a grand feeling of wind roaring over the earth and crashing through the tops of the trees in this—

> Not long the silence followed:
> The voice that issues from the breast
> O glorious South-west.
> Along the gloom-horizon holloa'd;
> Warning the valleys with a mellow roar
> Thro' flapping wings; then sharp the woodland bore
> A shudder, and a noise of hands:
> A thousand horns from some far vale
> In ambush sounding on the gale.
> Forth from the cloven sky came bands
> Of revel-gathering spirits; trooping down,
> Some rode the tree-tops; some, on torn cloud-strips,
> Burst screaming through the lighted town:
> And scudding seaward, some fell on big ships:
> Or mounting the sea-horses blew
> Bright foam-flakes on the black review
> Of heaving hulls and burying beaks.[2]

But such a method of progression is apt to become singularly like a catalogue, and I shall not follow it further. I have by this time tried to show sufficiently the scope

---
[1] *Night of Frost in May.*
[2] *Ode to the Spirit of Earth in Autumn.*

and plan of Meredith's writings on nature. In these two chapters I have tried to trace some of the thoughts he has had upon her philosophy and beauty. As I said before we cannot really separate these two ideas. They are merged together by the very nature of the subject, and the foundation of each is the inspiration of the other. Nature means to Meredith the elemental power that is around us, seen in its myriad lives in every aspect of loveliness and solemnity. The philosophy of nature is the lesson of existence, and the beauty of nature is the assurance of an ideal. He has endeavoured to read the great mother of us all and grasp some fragment of her mystic page. For he has seen that nature has to be followed in the main, and that therefore the clearer we understand her, the surer will be our footing. We obey her not only because she is beneficent, but because she is all-mighty. Sanity and advance are in the path of obedience, madness and decay in the path of disobedience. The glow of a sunset is the glow of a divine reality, not the gleam of an insane hallucination; the philosophy of nature is the lesson of a living wisdom, not the hopeless warning of a drunken and purposeless mechanism.

CHAPTER V

Philosophic Conception of Social Problems

THE problems of society are not such as find a perfect solution in our present civilization. The position of the individual to the community and the rights of personality present themselves to everybody in fresh aspects. It is becoming more and more plain that conduct is largely founded upon dogmas of questionable value, and that such words as morality and justice are capable of interpretations far different from those of the law and common usage. I do not mean that the present readings of these words are necessarily wrong, but that there is all over an awakened feeling that they may be wrong—that, in fact, the knowledge on which they are founded is itself uncertain. Is conduct merely a matter of the evolution of society, a method of making life livable, or is it based upon an inherent comprehension of the absolutely good ? Are we bound to sacrifice ourselves for society, or is the individual (who indeed goes to form society) to live out his individuality?

People are apt to label themselves under extreme titles, such as socialist, individualist, statu-quo-ite and so forth, but we know very well that existence is largely a matter of compromise, and that we find the forces of any one side frequently ranged under the banners of the other.

But indeed there are questions on which each personality throws anew a keen and searching light, questions which vitally affect conduct and which are bound to assert themselves. My object in this chapter is to see what is Meredith's general attitude towards these things, not going into minute detail, but rather into the spirit in which he had conceived them and the attitude of mind in which he has thought out these phases of life and philosophy.

First of all then there is the burning problem of the relation of the individual to society. There can be no shelving of this: every man and woman has it thrust before him or her, and they must decide for themselves what they will do. Our modern literary psychologists have girded themselves to fight it out to the end. Ibsen, the greatest of his school, is filled with a tragic sense of the isolation of personality, and would tell us that in the very fact of our possessing personalities we stand utterly alone and are inherently no less the victims of ourselves than the conquerors of the world. There is no compromise about Ibsen—he is an individualist pure and simple. I have seen it said somewhere that his psychology tended to lead him into pathology, and I think that in the gloomy studies of his later days there is some ground for the remark, but undoubtedly he is a most suggestive and masterly thinker. I mention him specially because in this very position he offers an interesting contrast to Meredith. Ibsen is an extremist, and the more he believes he is right, the more terrible is the price he makes his characters pay for this belief. Meredith, though perfectly clear as to what he thinks the true course, is nevertheless quite sane, and philosophical in a practical way, never losing sight of actual existence in his theories, and consequently never losing grip of progress through a medium of optimism. I admit of course that temperament is largely at the root of these differences, but after all, temperament is itself a weapon in the armoury of the brain. However revolutionary Meredith may be, he never fails to realize that the other side also has a cause. He has a strong and profound belief in advance by means of society. Perhaps in his poems this is even more strikingly and directly impressed than in his novels, though in the famous epistle of Dr Shrapnel in *Beauchamp's Career*,[1] there is an expression of it, not at all ambiguous. He believes that civilization is held together by society, and that no general forward movement is possible save in the van of civilization. His whole philosophy of living for the generations that are to come tends to intensify this attitude. Personality seems to him not so important as the aims of personality—the one dying, the other lasting for ever. But it cannot be argued that he is against individual freedom. He simply lays stress upon the fact that freedom is itself governed by certain laws. The main characters in his books are people energetically exercising a pronounced freedom of action, and we can notice that they have his sympathy. He is not a socialist, he is a philosophic radical.

The marriage question again is one of these difficulties on which he has thought long and with sensible originality. It is in a way

[1] Chap. xxix.

an epitome of the whole relationship of the sexes. Nothing could well be supposed more complicated than the intricacies of this subject. To the happily married, the position of the doubter is perhaps incomprehensible, but to the unhappily married it resolves itself with vehemence into the old question of the individual versus society. In the midst of all the talk about socialism, people are becoming ever more filled with strange and new self-consciousness and fine chords of individual perception, which tend to drive them in upon themselves to argue the great insolubles and search out the meanings and nuances of life. We are in the age of the questioner, and are no longer content to take our ethics from ancient custom. The whole question of marriage is one of absorbing importance, and one that has become to Meredith perhaps the most gigantic of the problems that the philosophy of conduct has to face. His three last novels are eloquent sermons on this text. *One of Our Conquerors* tells of a man who marries a woman much older than himself, and then leaves her for the woman he should have married: *Lord Ormont and his Aminta* is the story of a woman who married a man far her senior, and then leaves him when the true lover comes; *The Amazing Marriage* narrates the tale of a hasty marriage and the tragic sequel. But though these are the three stories that most directly touch upon the subject, it is one that he has always been considering. Indeed it is the one astounding problem, for which society uses the plain explanation that it is the basis of Society, formed by society, and the one step to consolidated civilization; and the individual, the equally plain answer, that as such it is good, but in its possible and frequent hardships it is utterly and irretrievably merciless, Meredith sees both positions. Briefly he would say to those on whom the law tramples, 'I realize your view—you are right to act as free agents if you wish to, but remember this, you have no right to complain if society casts you out, for you have offended society. in which you are only a unit of the great whole.' The idea of life is to make it harmonious with its environment, or if you like to put it so, the environment harmonious with the life. Every one must be allowed to work out the questions of existence for himself. To be shocked or alarmed by the incongruity of other minds to your own is frequently a misunderstanding of what is liberty, personality, and even happiness. Intellectual anarchists are not necessarily out of touch with nature, though they are not necessarily in touch with it. Most people violently declaim that they are either the one or the other. Society has demands upon us, but we also have demands upon ourselves. Happy marriages are very numerous, which would seem to show that it is as at present constituted an inspired institution, but unhappy marriages are also very numerous, which would seem to show something very much the reverse. Some would say that the strictness of the divorce laws is the saviour of the situation, some again that the strictness of these laws is an obvious scandal. The shuttlecock of feeling will continue, as far as can be seen, for centuries to come. Daily is life becoming more complicated, not less outwardly than in the machinery of the emotions. What is morality? what is progress? what is truth? Such questions are being asked, and every one is giving a different answer. Meredith seems to say with no uncertain voice, 'Follow what nature and nature's human assistant, society, dictate, but follow them only to the point where Individuality will naturally merge itself in their flow. Beware lest you lose your will, for it is only through a conjunction of will and nature that any safe footing can be reached.'

The position of women, too, is a matter on which he has uttered no lukewarm sentiment. A half civilized orientalism is still at the root of our treatment of her, appearing truly enough behind a veneer of emancipation. His ironical remark, (put into the mouth of Diana)

'Men may have rounded Seraglio Point: they have not yet doubled Cape Turk'[1]

signifies that although we no longer treat her outwardly as Easterns, still in our hearts she is not an equal. A perfervid politeness only tends to emphasize this. Meredith holds that in all the essentials of a thinking intellect, woman is not only not inferior to man, but even gifted with a finer innate perception of many of life's problems. On the splendid gallery of women he has pictured, he has expended all the wealth of care and imagination that should bring into the light his opinions of their inherent nobility. He has long been an apostle of the equality of the sexes, not merely as a theoretical truth, but as a thing that should be carried out in the civil government of the country. He does not believe that society can throw off the

[1] *Diana of the Crossways*, chap. i.

last relic of barbarism until the footing of all those who form society shall be, at any rate in the eyes of the law, the same. Real progress is alone possible where an understanding of what is the true basis on which society ought to be founded, has been finally settled. Despotism of any description is always reactionary in the long run, and one of the chief things in any injustice is to make people realize what is the foundation of justice. If a doctor knows that a man's only chance of recovery is to take a certain medicine, it is his duty to make this apparent to the patient whatever opposition he may encounter from the patient himself. Facts seem sometimes to paralyse theories, but there are some theories so great that they are simply an exalted way of looking at facts. In all Meredith's novels we see one point plainly insisted on, and it is this, that despite of certain weak spots in the feminine outlook, still it is an outlook innately claiming by its very equipment, both feeble and strong, a far larger measure of justice and equality than has hitherto been its lot. If we were to take the matter simply from the extraordinarily egoistic position of very many men (which is infinitely removed from Meredith's position), we might come still to the same conclusion, by owning that education is only possible where education is given, and that knowledge is the result of opportunity.

His attitude towards politics is also one in which he shows a strong feeling of enlivened common sense. The democratic ideal has to be tempered by a comprehension of facts, and the probable, as well as the desirable future to which they may lead us. But the quick brain here once more grasps a danger of sinking into the quagmire of old platitude. Nothing is so easy as to say it must be so, therefore let it be; and there is always a time when facts are moulded by men over and above the constant moulding of evolution. His teaching is really that of cautious, but decided and wakeful advance—cautious in that there is a law of caution all through nature, decided and wakeful in that human beings are apt to slumber in the light of that knowledge. For there is an element of personality that claims something and will work out something, and for understanding of which little if any lesson can be gained through a philosophy of unhuman nature. A large view is needed in politics, and a mind intolerant of abuses, but tolerant of men as men. Only such a one can fully grasp how much is in a state of transition, and how much of everyday life and even of strange and unjust deeds is the outcome of far wider issues, far more primal passions, than the occasion would seem to suggest or the action seem to warrant.

And observe another reform for which he holds a constant and eloquent plea. He sees minds in general sunk in a dismal mass of triviality. There is no tangible aim in anything, and existence is resolving itself into patterns of yesterday and emotional attempts to forecast a still more unremunerative future. There is not a definite thought and philosophy in the brain of the people; and life, beginning to free itself from the influence of superstition, is finding itself without that last ideal that did at least make it have a meaning coherent in its very vagueness. Meredith has realized the frightful canker of perpetual trifling. Poetry, which is the breath of hope, must die out in minds that are the epitome of a suburb. Sin may destroy the individual, but it is mediocrity that will kill the world. All his books are essays written to show the reverse of this. They are attempts to make life really a living thing and personality an actual constituent of romance. There is something most deeply tragic in these grand words—

> Cold as a mountain in its star-pitched tent,
> Stood high Philosophy, less friend than foe :
> Whom self-caged Passion, from its prison-bars,
> Is always watching with a wondering hate.
> Not till the fire is dying in the grate,
> Look we for any kinship with the stars.[1]

How darkly are our thoughts encompassed by the passions of the earth, and how easily do we let slip from us the influence of our origin. The calm and buoyant outlook of philosophy is drowned in weeping and hope is extinguished by a flood of tears. Life to many is simply an unhappy and horrible delusion, where everything is a meaningless enigma and passions kindle, only to consume, the soul. Not till certain hollow echoes mournfully rolling through the spaces of the brain begin to tell us that time's future is blank and the hour is at hand, not till then 'look we for any kinship with the stars.'

But as I said at the beginning it is not so much with Meredith's way of looking at particular social problems that I wish to deal, as with the atmosphere in which he has considered them as a whole. I have given

[1] *Modern Love*, stanza iv.

very shortly a few typical instances, but they must only be taken as such, and more as examples than real examinations. The chief point is this, that he has had before him in treating of all these things a true and consistent outlook. Whenever we find a man striving through a whole lifetime to press home to us a view of the world which in all the diversity of its judgments is still visible as an harmonious scheme, then we may be sure that he has something to tell us to which it is worth listening. In Meredith we feel strongly an unswerving philosophy of conduct. I do not mean of course that every question finds a sure and ready answer, or indeed that he never seems to contradict himself, but that every question is tested by the abstract laws that have formed his personality and his opinions. Words like justice and liberty do not merely convey to him one method of considering life, they actually are life. As I mentioned before, where he would sometimes seem to differ from the most ardent disciples of freedom is in his philosophic grasp of the fact that freedom is itself subject to laws. But in such books as *Vittoria* and *Beauchamp's Career*, and in many characters and many scenes throughout all his books, there is a constant and passionate appeal for freedom and the claims of the individual. He admits that it is through society progress must be made, but he does not lose sight of the truth that society is comprised of individuals, and that there is in personal liberty a sense of something not less sacred than mysterious.

CHAPTER VI

Insight into Character

I PROPOSE in this chapter to examine Meredith's insight into character, to explain, that is to say, some of those dramatic and sympathetic points which effectually define the strength of the novelist. For profound and accurate delineation of motive and personality are essential to the novelist of psychology. He has to see ideals struggling for outlet in characters devoid of commanding power of expression, and at the same time to realize the actual differences of outlook that are at the base of individuality. He must make his creations live, but he cannot help tingeing them with his own atmosphere. Every dramatist and every novelist must to some extent represent himself or his ideas in his figures, for they are all the children of one brain. Meredith, for instance, has cast over all his characters a light of poetry. They are built of that 'auroral' air of which Mr William Sharp speaks in his fine article on 'The Country of George Meredith', in the *Pall Mall Magazine* for May, 1904. They are all, as I said in my introduction, types of humanity. He reads them not only in the realistic atmosphere of fact, but in the elusive atmosphere of idealism. He gathers into each figure the conception he has of such a type. And it is not the case that this method destroys the actuality of the picture. On the contrary, it is vividly real, breathing, living, because it is simply the author faithfully transcribing his white-hot imagining of himself under all the conditions that form another. I do not suppose that anyone has had a more subtle insight into character or has more clearly read the dim language of personality. His creations are largely intuitive perceptions of types, and live in themselves as representatives of actual phases. Keen intellectual observation, joined to this innate sympathetic understanding and poetical idealization, have given him the secret of his searching analysis. His portraits live, but they are typical of what we instinctively feel is the greatness of the type. In fact, we see in them the touch of the universal, which, after all, is the highest standard of reality. They are not mirrors of an age, they are mirrors of an ideal. They dwell in an atmosphere that is not local, but still each of them passes an actual life with the kind of mind easily comprehended as actual in the circumstances. They cover their real destinies, obviously helped by no knowledge of their immortality. We observe them as ideals, but there is not an impossible strain to make them such, and they are not only not incongruous, but most apparently part of a moving drama.

The truth is, that each figure is typical of the atmosphere in which it moves. In fact it is only when it is otherwise that we get a shock of unreality.

But of course all these generalities are of no value at all without a rather close examination of the characters, and of the surroundings in which they play their parts. There lies the whole proof of the truth or otherwise of the contention. And before entering on this I would once more urge you to recall to your minds the typical atmosphere of Meredith's books. It is most essential that we do not forget that these novels are written by a philosopher, a lyric poet, a humorist, and an observer with a secure and intense knowledge of our natures. It is such a combination that has produced these works, and which obviously is not likely to lay itself open to the ordinary pitfalls of the novelist. If we truly realize all this and, at the same time, the naturally strong individuality of such a creative mind, we shall not feel a sense of bewilderment in the face of his studies of character. Remember, they speak to us from the level of a complex intelligence. I do not mean that they are in themselves more obscure than ordinary people, but only that they are seen from more intricate and more mental standpoints. Meredith has seen that true understanding of character is to be read in niceties. In the questions and problems that ceaselessly ebb and flow within ourselves, in the strange, internal conflicts, in the unheard cries of individuality, he notes the emergence of a soul. Though he sees us dyed in the common dyes of sex, race, station, he sees that we are isolated and alone. As he says—

Character must ever be a mystery, only to be explained in some degree by conduct . .[1]

He has the amazing power of understanding other people from their own positions. He feels instinctively the battle that is the eternal

[1] *The Amazing Marriage*, chap. xlvii.

INSIGHT INTO CHARACTER

justification of each individuality. He has grasped what must seem a truism, but what has not apparently been grasped by many, that people seem real because they *are* real and have a real personality and point of view. Consequently there are few writers who have given such a splendid air of truth to their creations. And yet, as I have said, there is always about them an idealized atmosphere, a philosophic perception of their universality. In fact the first and last word on them is this, that they are types, and, as such, truer than the closest actuality.

In judging then of Meredith's power of character reading, we may first of all consider some of his special remarks in regard to character in general, and secondly pick out certain particular figures and trace with fairly elaborate detail the thread and current of their personalities.

Meredith, in one of the aphorisms of ' The Pilgrim's Scrip ' pierces to the reason of the lifelessness of most character study—

> The reason why men and women are mysterious to us, and prove disappointing, is that we will read them from our own book ; just as we are perplexed by reading ourselves from theirs.[1]

---

[1] *The Ordeal of Richard Feverel*, chap. xxix

It is the comprehension of this need that has given to even his abstract remarks on the subject a vitality and insight that show a mind actually faced with the problems which face the various personalities it creates. He sees in every person certain traits of character, each with its special application to that character, but each extraordinarily common under different disguises—so much so indeed that an impersonal generalization may be made from actions seemingly purely individual and suitable to a particular occasion. There are in fact few methods of more minutely examining the subtleties of abstract character than by the aphorism as wielded by Meredith. It seems to carry with it a comprehension of individual fitness and at the same time a sense of universal truth. Instances may be given by such remarks as these—

> There is nothing so indicative of fevered or of bad blood as the tendency to counsel the Almighty how he shall deal with his creatures.[1]

> For one curious operation of the charge of guiltiness upon the nearly guiltless is to make them paint themselves pure white, to the obliteration of minor spots, until the whiteness being acknowledged, or the ordeal imminent, the spots recur and press upon their consciences.[2]

---

[1] *Rhoda Fleming*, Chap. xliv.
[2] *Diana of the Crossways*, chap. xiv.

INSIGHT INTO CHARACTER 125

It will be found a common case, that when we have yielded to our instincts, and then have to soothe conscience, we must slaughter somebody, for a sacrificial offering to our sense of comfort.[1]

... she spoke with the desperate firmness of weak creatures that strive to nail themselves to the sound of it.[2]

There is pain in the surrendering of that we are fain to relinquish.[3]

Surely there is in these sentences a delicate and true insight to phases that are both personal and at the same time common to everyone.

He has also great penetration to unfold certain universal traits of the two sexes, traits which at different ages and in different figures may show more clearly above the surface, but which are truly typical. How well we can note, for instance, the spirit of male egoism, sometimes most clearly demonstrated as in Sir Austin Feverel,[4] Sir Willoughby Patterne,[5] Victor Radnor;[6] many times in less entire obviousness—Lord Ormont,[7]

---

[1] *Beauchamp's Career*, chap. xii.
[2] *The Tragic Comedians*, chap. viii.
[3] *The Egoist*, chap. xiv.
[4] *The Ordeal of Richard Feverel.*
[5] *The Egoist.*
[6] *One of our Conquerors.*
[7] *Lord Ormont and his Aminta.*

Lord Fleetwood,[1] and literally a score of others suggest themselves. We can put our hand upon this line of egoism in a hundred characters, in all of them an individual and subtle strain as modified by their personalities and surroundings, in all of them a universal point of the masculine mind. And there are more elusive but not less representative points to be noted. For instance, the following seems to me a remark, the clear insight of which it is almost impossible to exaggerate—

> A profound belief in the efficacy of his eloquence, when he chose to expend it, was one of the principal supports of Edward's sense of mastery;—a secret sense belonging to certain men in every station of life, and which is the staff of many an otherwise impressible and fluctuating intellect.[2]

It is simply a completely true remark, laying bare a facet of the minds of young men with such power of acute perception that those to whom they may have been until now a mystery will not unlikely find here the perfect clue. This is almost another way of saying the same thing—

> He closed, as it were, a black volume, and opened a new and a bright one. Young men easily fancy that

---

[1] *The Amazing Marriage.*
[2] *Rhoda Fleming,* chap. xxxvii.

INSIGHT INTO CHARACTER

they may do this, and that when the black volume is shut the tide is stopped. Saying 'I was a fool,' they believe they have put an end to the foolishness. What father teaches them that a human act once set in motion flows on for ever to the great account? Our deathlessness is in what we do, not in what we are. Comfortable youth thinks otherwise.[1]

More obvious, undoubtedly, is the insight of the following remark, but here again, the stamp is the stamp of actuality—

You are aware that men's faith in a woman whom her sisters discountenance, and partially repudiate, is uneasy, however deeply they may be charmed. On the other hand, she may be guilty of prodigious oddities without much disturbing their reverence, while she is in the feminine circle.[2]

There will be found in Meredith's portraits of men, in all the ramifications of their personalities, the peculiar dividing into stages of growth which is very observable in real life. The boy, the man of twenty to twenty-five, the man of thirty to thirty-five, the middle-aged man, the old man—they are all suggested with a uniformity of matter-of-factness that shows the touch of a master. I do not propose to try to define his general method of representing these ages, but it is true that each one is, in his grasp, really

[1] *Rhoda Fleming*, chap. xvi.
[2] *Rhoda Fleming*, chap. xxi.

typical of that certain mental atmosphere that goes with each period. This is the marvellous fact—the life-like accuracy of the atmosphere of the personality, and the atmosphere of the impersonal side, the age, the sex, the class, etc. He seems able to gauge accurately the general aspect towards life that does really accompany each stage of life, quite apart from the personality of the character. Adding to this, keen and balanced touches to show their individual existence, he creates figures of flesh and blood. Many novelists can create mental figures, very few, figures that really live. For most novelists are intent upon making their creations individual as individuals and nothing else, instead of making them also individual as people of a certain age, sex, time, environment, position and all the other points that compose the impersonal individuality of a man or a woman. They imagine it would seem, that the first must embrace the second, but it is really a totally inaccurate supposition, as far as any artistic completeness of portraiture is concerned.

It is easy enough to see what types have the sympathy or admiration of Meredith, though it is rather noticeable that he has very seldom attempted to draw characters of commanding intellectual power. An essential manliness is demanded by him. This is really the word that epitomizes his creed. Sentimentalism or sham in any form is abhorrent to him, as also indeed is acute egoism, though for this he has a far more lenient eye, realizing no doubt its diverse universality and even naturalness. True enthusiasts deeply interest him, especially when it is the case of a mental attitude at war with its environment. In fact all show of disinterested and chivalrous individualism has his respect. The racy strength of the soil always appeals to him and wins a very just acknowledgment. But of all the different types he has imagined, the most near to his true idea of manhood would seem to be that set forth in such figures as Merthyr Powys,[1] Vernon Whitford,[2] Tom Redworth,[3] Matey Weyburn,[4]—strong, quiet men of action. In them he sums up the ' divine average ' that sanity aspires to. They are to him as men, what Vittoria,[5]

[1] *Sandra Belloni* and *Vittoria*.
[2] *The Egoist*.
[3] *Diana of the Crossways*.
[4] *Lord Ormont and his Aminta*.
[5] *Sandra Belloni* and *Vittoria*.

Nesta Radnor,[1] Jenny Denham,[2] and numerous others, are as women. I do not mean that the personalities of such men and women can be compared, but that in their instinctive completeness and dignity they come close to one another.

Let us pass now to a consideration of Meredith's knowledge of women, which for several reasons seems even more notable than his knowledge of men : firstly because a man's understanding of women must appear more remarkable than a man's understanding of men ; secondly, because he really does appear to have brought in most cases a finer analysis to bear on women than men ; and thirdly, because the inherent feminine nature more strikingly develops under such an examination. For women are on the whole more truly under the sway of their impersonal individuality than men. It is not that they are easier to understand—they are harder—but that they all cease to be comprehensible at certain clearly seen points. A man always knows that he will cease to understand a woman and when, a woman may understand a man to his very last

[1] *One of our Conquerors.*
[2] *Beauchamp's Career.*

INSIGHT INTO CHARACTER

turning. Meredith, with almost tragic insight, has followed the track of women along the intricate path of their inborn nature. Where the ordinary man says, 'Here she ceases to be comprehensible,' he says, 'Here she becomes truly woman'—that is to say, typical of innate womanhood. An acute and cordial sympathy leads him forward. It is this that has given him the understanding of the high ideal of womanhood so nobly presented in many portraits. I do not propose to make a list of all these great and memorable types, and to name only a selection would be a double injustice, but to anyone who knows his works it must be entirely unnecessary. They are studies in the highest sense, full of poetry, fire, imagination, and the splendour of physical and mental beauty. They are intensely human and embodiments of the profoundly questioning and progressive spirit of true womanhood. As he says—

There is the democratic virus secret in every woman . . [1]

For it is at the ideal he is arriving, through all the weakness and decay; not that he would have them unearthly, far from it, but that he sees through all the trammels of earth,

[1] *Rhoda Fleming*, chap. xxii.

132 INSIGHT INTO CHARACTER

the divinity that springs from earth. With an astonishing and unique sureness of perception he has seen the universal mental outlook so logically misunderstood by men. Their weak armour at certain crises is clearly observed, as in such a remark as the following—

> He committed the capital fault of treating her as his equal in passion and courage, not as metal ready to run into the mould under temporary stress of fire.[1]

and the perpetually baffling obscurity of their psychology under any emotional strain. The character studies of Mrs Culling [2] and Mrs Victor Radnor [3] are profound instances. Here also is a sentence that needs no comment—

> 'He tries to be more than he is,' thought the lady: and began insensibly to conceive him less than he was.[4]

It may be added here that Meredith is very successful in the portrayal of the middle-aged, rich, aristocratically-eccentric woman of the world. Examples such as Lady Jocelyn,[5] Lady Gosstre,[6] Mrs Mountstuart Jenkinson,[7] Baroness von Crefeldt,[8] Lady

---

[1] *Beauchamp's Career*, chap. ix.
[2] *Beauchamp's Career*.   [3] *One of our Conquerors*.
[4] *The Ordeal of Richard Feverel*, chap. xxxvii.
[5] *Evan Harrington*.   [6] *Sandra Belloni*.
[7] *The Egoist*.
[8] *The Tragic Comedians*.

INSIGHT INTO CHARACTER

Charlotte Eglett[1] and many more are forthcoming. It is a type for which he has a peculiar affection, and into whose mouth he places many of his witty and scintillating remarks upon society. He likes their calm sense of mastery and ease, and their aristocratic independence of judgment and freedom of action and opinion.

Meredith constantly draws attention to man's attitude to women. There is the famous aphorism in 'The Pilgrim's Scrip', in which he says—

> I expect that Woman will be the last thing civilized by Man.[2]

and sums up once and for all the firm belief of countless men, which they endeavour to hide vainly enough under an elegant show of refined courtliness. More crudely put but pointing equally to the same conclusion is this—

> His ejaculation 'Women!' was, as he knew, merely ignorance roaring behind a mask of sarcasm.[3]

It arises from a fatal misconception of the whole basic outlook of the feminine mind, or perhaps rather from an acknowledgment

---
[1] *Lord Ormont and His Aminta.*
[2] *The Ordeal of Richard Feverel*, chap. i.
[3] *Lord Ormont and His Aminta*, chap. xii.

that it is an outlook hopelessly beyond their comprehension. It is Meredith, I say, who has pierced beyond this sluggish acceptance of defeat, and sought in the brain itself the reason and the meaning. With that double knowledge of which I spoke before, he loses no sight of the inherent individuality of the sex. It is this knowledge that has helped him so greatly when in the dimmer fields of motive and character. I do not know how it would be possible to make a much truer remark than the following—

> She had gone through her crisis in the anticipation of it. That is how quick natures will often be cold and hard, or not much moved, when the positive crisis arrives, and why it is that they are prepared for astonishing leaps over the gradations which should render their conduct comprehensible to us, if not excusable.[1]

It shows insight of a very remarkable order.

Now it must be quite apparent that such a mind grasps not only the good, which here really means the natural, but also the bad, which is the untrue and the false. There are few people Meredith is more totally out of sympathy with than the women with whom he does not sympathise. The Constance

[1] *The Egoist*, chap. xxi.

INSIGHT INTO CHARACTER

Aspers,[1] the Lady Wathins,[2] leave him more than cold; the sentimentalists gain little from him. Such a remark as this is extremely cutting—

> Despair, I have said before, is a wilful business, common to corrupt blood, and to weak woeful minds: native to the sentimentalist of the better order.[3]

But notice how different is his treatment of women whom one might well suppose approximated in worthlessness to the two already mentioned, if only they are at heart human, therefore real. I am thinking now of the three Pole girls [4] and of the Countess de Saldar.[5] They are apparently utterly false to fine ideals of womanhood, and yet underneath the surface this is by no means the case. Over and over again their actuality springs up, and we see them before us as living women. It is when the mind is false as well as the cultivated attitude, that Meredith loses the last trace of sympathy and draws for us those grotesquely-accurate similitudes of women.

Having then tried to define some of Meredith's typical ideas of men and women, it will

[1,2] *Diana of the Crossways.*
[3] *Sandra Belloni*, chap. xxxviii
[4] *Sandra Belloni.*
[5] *Evan Harrington.*

be a good thing to study a few of his figures in the light of their actual existence. By tracing their mental development we gain the truest sense of his power of reading aright the tangled scroll of individuality : by watching them evolve through their instincts and natural resources we see the wisdom and reality of his observation. For it is only when brought face to face with life, that the abstractions that explain personality begin to glow with the fire of actuality. Besides, in character-drawing, there can be, as we know, an extraordinary sense of atmosphere, spreading a feeling of truth over the picture, which of course it is quite impossible to present in impersonal truisms, or in fact even to any extent in such an examination as I am now proposing. Well, then, the question remains, which out of all the immense gallery of portraits are we to choose for the purposes of this fuller consideration. For undoubtedly the standard of selection is remarkable. Meredith's figures are always individual and striking, they are always notably true to themselves. Another difficulty in selecting typical examples is the fact that many of the characters are tinged with an inborn eccentricity, which is invariably most difficult to explain in logical progression. Men like Richmond Roy are fascinating, but to most people there is about them a gleam of the greenish fire of madness. True enough they are sane in so far as we can comprehend their actions if only we can once allow the possibility of their existence. I myself strongly believe in the truth of such pictures, but I admit their basic position is practically impossible of explanation. A strong touch of wandering romance has inclined Meredith to such creations, just as it has caused him to dwell lovingly on the splendour of success and on romantic and startling positions.

Perhaps there are no more suitable figures for our purpose than those of Nevil Beauchamp,[1] Sir Willoughby Patterne,[2] Sandra Belloni,[3] and Diana Warwick.[4] These four seem to me very representative of his general imaginative grasp of personality and of the problems that surround humanity from day to day. A book of length might very well be written on the people of George Meredith's novels. I cannot even begin to mention the

---

[1] *Beauchamp's Career.*
[2] *The Egoist.*
[3] *Sandra Belloni* and *Vittoria.*
[4] *Diana of the Crossways.*

characteristic names that I am compelled to omit, but I am convinced that no complete knowledge of his mind and philosophy can be acquired without a careful study of them and of the surroundings and circumstances that summoned them forward on the track.

Nevil Beauchamp is one of these enthusiasts whose impetuosity is only equalled by their logic. The very first incident of his career—the writing of a letter to the French army on the subject of a slight to England—though ridiculous enough, is nevertheless full of a serious spirit of logical patriotism. It is a boy's idea, but in it is the germ of the future. Next he comes under the sway of Carlyle's teaching and finds in him the well-spring of all his forming opinions. He becomes mentally an idealist and consequently a questioner of all the civilization and social conditions of his time. Meanwhile, as an officer in the navy he has taken part in the Crimean war, been invalided in Venice, fallen in love with a French girl, and endeavoured, almost successfully, to make her fly with him. During the next few years he is on the coast of Africa and in the Mediterranean. On returning to England he happens to hear a democratic doctor make

INSIGHT INTO CHARACTER

a political speech, and within two hours of landing has settled with him to become the radical candidate for the very borough round which are the seats of his uncle and friends. In all these actions, though mentioned here in the baldest possible way, we see the three leading traits of his life—patriotism, impetuous enthusiasm, logic. His bravery in the Crimea, his volunteering for service on the deadly West Coast, his deep thoughts for the welfare of the people, are the tests of patriotism. For the other two, see what his action shows. He says in so many words to the girl, 'We love each other, therefore let us fly together and get married, and let us do so at once whilst we have the opportunity, or you will be compelled to marry someone you dislike and we will both be miserable': he says in so many words to himself, 'This man has convinced me that what he advocates is the only thing for these people. I can volunteer to help and therefore I will, and at once.'

It is from this stage that the analysis of his life and personality really begin, and consequently it is just at this stage that the impossibility of summarizing his life begins. For from here there seriously and fatefully begin to thread into it other lives. The position becomes more complex, and we are to watch in him the fights that are in the mind and the conscience. Briefly speaking there are three main things that sway the crucial months of his life. First his love affairs, secondly his endeavours to get his uncle to apologise to Dr Shrapnel for wrongly assaulting him, thirdly his social and political dreams.

Nevil Beauchamp's love affairs are of that kind that border on a strange impersonalism. The idealism in him creates types that arise from his impressions of actual people, and immediately soar beyond the actuality—again a trait, typical of his nature. Only to theories and to the logical carrying out of them can he summon absolute enthusiasm. His encounters with his uncle are points in fact. The desire for justice mixed with a passionate longing to explain the greatness of the doctor's teaching spur him to untiring and most earnest endeavours. The feeling of being in the right and of yet being unable even to make anyone admit the possible rightness of his thesis is finely rendered in the kind of blank astonishment of some of his conversations.

Another point about him, and one Meredith especially lays stress on, is his absolute lack of Byronism. There is in him no conceit, none of the poseur. He has been called a modern Gracchus and there is much truth in the epithet. He is an extremely sane person and an extremely sincere one, and he is a born aristocrat, filled with the innate culture of the aristocrat. We see in this the opening for his mental battles. He is for ever being faced with problems, on each side of which there seems a reasonable answer. The clue to at least partially understanding him, is in the fact that he is an idealist of the democratic type, whose ideas are not only logical in theory, as the ideas of all true idealists are, but carried out with a logical and modest conciseness of action which it is somehow difficult to associate with this kind of mind. As I say, there is nothing histrionic or even vague about Beauchamp. He actually is endowed with noble and aspiring hopes and a personality not less magnetic than great. In my chapter on tragedy I have given the description of his death as perhaps the finest piece of tragic writing in the whole range of Meredithian prose. I need only say here that the heroic atmosphere of these sentences is undoubtedly Meredith's own description of the value of the aims and personality of Beauchamp himself. It would be hard to imagine any man more hopelessly and fundamentally different from Nevil Beauchamp than Sir Willoughby Patterne—the Egoist. He is the incarnation of the spirit of ordered things and the representative of the modern conservatism of the county magnate. Sir Willoughby is a baronet, who, whilst still a child, has come into his heritage—a title, a great fortune, and a position of power in his county. From his earliest youth he is made fully aware of all this. In surroundings of almost abject flattery, he grows to consider himself a king, whose will there is not only compunction but longing to obey. It is obvious that there was born in him a vein of excessive egoism, but it is certainly true that few up-bringings could have more admirably developed it.

The unfolding of Sir Willoughby's character is shown mainly in his relations to women. He becomes engaged to a famous beauty, who, on the eve of marriage, elopes with a cavalry officer. Sir Willoughby retires into the expressionless depths of wounded self-love. He makes no outward sign of the blow, but immediately and openly pays great attention to a Miss Dale, whose father has a house on his estate. Thus he attempts to guard himself from the scandal of the county, by proving that he himself was only too thankful for the step—and was he not perhaps the subtle prompter of it? Leaving Miss Dale in the fluttering spirit of the indecisive-obvious, Sir Willoughby betakes himself on a tour round the world. He is absent for several years and returns to renew warmly his acquaintance with her, but with no word of a proposal or even suggestion of it. In him, we must remember there is the double egoism, or is it perhaps merely the refined completeness of egoism, which tries not only to rule outwardly but to satisfy the sentimental desire for an inward comfort. This is the secret of his renewed warmth to Miss Dale. He does not intend to marry her, but he cannot bear to think that she should no longer reverence and worship him as fully as of old.

The county is next thrilled by the announcement of his engagement to a Miss Clara Middleton, the daughter of a rich and worldly cleric. The girl comes with her father to stay with Sir Willoughby, and it is the gradual opening of her eyes to his character and her desperate attempts to break off her engagement, round which the whole story and analysis of motive really hang. Little by little he all unconsciously unfolds his mind before her. He declines to take back a servant who has left him, because he will not acknowledge the right of anyone to even possess a thought of voluntarily leaving him. There is a kind of abstraction in him that it is impossible to fathom. He will argue matters with people freely enough to a certain point, but there is in his mind a sort of holy of holies, from whence he looks at everything with a sense of finality that precludes argument. And with all this, he is a man of the most acute sensibility. It is his aim to be the perfect great man of the county, and his life is balanced to achieve this. The thought of anyone laughing at him, or even discussing him, is agony. He is in the constant state of testing the sureness of his position and of gratifying the deep-rooted and inordinate vanity of the egoist. Here for instance, in a conversation with Miss Dale, is a telling illustration of this—

' And you are well ? ' The anxious question permitted him to read deeply in her eyes. He found the man he sought there, squeezed him passionately, and let her go . .[1]

---

[1] *The Egoist*, chap. iv.

INSIGHT INTO CHARACTER

But he carries his egoism to a depth of fatuity that becomes blind through the very desire to assure himself of the actuality of the esteem he is held in, or it may be perhaps that it is of so gross a kind that in real moments of a crisis it shows itself as totally swallowing all sense of decency. Read for instance this scene between Sir Willoughby and Clara Middleton—

'An oath?' she said, and moved her lips to recall what she might have said and forgotten. 'To what? what oath?'
'That you will be true to me dead as well as living? Whisper it.'
'Willoughby, I shall be true to my vows at the altar.'
'To me! me!'
'It will be to you.'
'To my soul. No heaven can be for me—I see none only torture, unless I have your word, Clara. I trust it, I will trust it implicitly. My confidence in you is absolute.'
'Then you need not be troubled.'
'It is for *you*, my love; that you may be armed and strong when I am not by to protect you.'
'Our views of the world are opposed, Willoughby.'
'Consent; gratify me; swear it. Say "Beyond death." Whisper it. I ask for nothing more. Women, think the husband's grave breaks the bond, cuts the tie, sets them loose. They wed the flesh—pah! What I call on you for is nobility, the transcendent nobility of faithfulness beyond death. "*His* widow!" let them say; a saint in widowhood.'[1]

---

[1] *The Egoist*, chap. vi.

It is not easy to picture anything more unclothed.

But as a rule Sir Willoughby is as Meredith says 'anything but obtuse'. I cannot give here any idea of the long struggle between him and Clara Middleton. If possible, he is determined to avoid the scandal and talk of the county and the wound to his own inmost self-love. The conflict is one developed through many chapters with paralysing subtlety of psychological detail. The whole unlovely mind of Sir Willoughby is dissected, and he is left as the shivering landmark of a perpetual example. He makes frantic efforts to retain her, flinging from him, either through inherent baseness or an absolute mania of self-pity (which is the reaction of egoism) the scruples of fair play. The whole episode of his instilling his influence into her father to gain him over to his side is of a colour almost too gloomy for comedy.[1] Nevertheless, he at length realizes that failure must result. We have seen him once before acting to Miss Dale as the unjust steward acted to certain creditors on a famous occasion—preparing another line of defence in case of disaster. And now again he falls

[1] *The Egoist,* chap. xx.

back upon her. He has that extraordinary but not uncommon nature, which ceases to desire what it sees totally impossible to obtain, and thinks it really does transfer true affection to suitable subjects at almost a moment's notice. It is the nature of the philosophic sentimentalist. But she too has had her eyes opened. Again he plays a part as selfish as it is cowardly. He dare not lose. He brings against her all the forces at his command. His two aunts, her invalid father, beseech her at midnight to become engaged to him. He behaves like one demented, raving of life-long love, eternal passion and so forth. Weary, disillusioned, she consents, and in a moment the agonized pleader becomes the polished suitor.

Sandra Belloni is without any doubt whatsoever one of the most magnetic and splendid figures in the novels of George Meredith. She is the daughter of an Italian refugee and an English mother. Her early life is spent in squalid poverty in London, and when one day she learns that she is to marry a Jewish money-lender, she immediately flies into the country without any ideas as to destination. By the merest chance she finds herself at a farm near the home of a certain city merchant and his three daughters, ladies who are ' scaling society by the help of the Arts '.[1]

It is here the story commences. The three Miss Poles and their brother Wilfrid and Antonio Pericles, a Greek of fabulous wealth, complete unscrupulousness, and a passion for music, hearing reports of a beautiful voice heard every evening in an adjoining wood, make an expedition in search of the marvel. They discover Sandra singing in the wood, and such an impression does she arouse, that all of them at once form plans of which she is the natural centre. Antonio resolves to have her voice trained in Italy, Wilfrid begins to fall in love with her, the three ladies settle that she is to stay with them to serve as a stepping-stone to a county reputation. She comes to their house, and it is whilst newly there she recounts to Wilfrid the story of her early career. It is very interesting to speculate on Sandra at this time. Her character is one of extraordinary naïveté and frankness, but behind there is clearly seen the reserve of womanhood. She is just on the verge of full mental growth. So much is this so that we can actually follow the development of her character. We can

[1] *Sandra Belloni*, chap i.

INSIGHT INTO CHARACTER 149

see her gradually rising away from the misty memories of her youth into a knowledge of the living reality of life. Wilfrid falls deeply in love with her and she with him. This is her full awakening. She is henceforth no longer a child, no longer a merely irresponsible follower of her whims. Sandra's character is that mixture of fire and steel, which is the foundation of the most noble personality. She loves with that passionate intensity of delicious strangeness which cannot imagine anything but the same mind in the loved one.

But Wilfrid Pole is of a calibre entirely different. His interests and his desires clash in a most awkward way, and he does his best to answer them both at once in a satisfactory manner. He is in fact a sentimental egoist of the worst kind. His interests suggest that he should become engaged to a lady of the county, his desires suggest that he should become engaged to Sandra Belloni. With admirable diplomacy he does both, wherein it is not difficult to see very great trouble not very far ahead. Here is what happens. Sandra is under promise to go to Italy at Mr Pericles' expense for the purpose of having her voice trained. She speaks to Wilfrid of this and entreats him to marry her soon in order that they may never be parted. He tries to soothe her in such a fashion as will not in the slightest degree compromise himself. Sandra, in a complete simplicity of heart, imagines that if Mr Pole would only give his consent, all difficulties would be at an end. She travels to London to unfold her mind to him. There is no doubt that at this time Mr Pole is slowly dying. All the symptoms are presented with graphic and even terrible power. His whirling brain can scarcely realize the position, and refuses for an instant to accept the situation. He knows that Wilfrid is already engaged to a lady of title, and can comprehend little else on the subject. His brutal frankness on first understanding anything is not the result of unkindness but of a confused and tired brain. As for Sandra she begins to be aware of dim meanings in his incoherent and disjointed phrases.

> She was too full of her own burning passion to take evidence from her sight. The sun of her world was threatened with extinction. She felt herself already a wanderer in the land of tombs, where none could say whether morning had come or gone. Intensely she looked her misery in the face; and it was as a voice that said, 'No sun; never sun any more,' to her. But a blue-hued moon slipped from among the clouds, and hung in the black out-stretched fingers of the tree of

INSIGHT INTO CHARACTER

darkness, fronting troubled waters. 'This is thy light for ever! thou shalt live in thy dream.' So, as in a prison-house, did her soul now recall the blissful hours by Wilming Weir. She sickened but an instant. The blood in her veins was too strong a tide for her to crouch in that imagined corpse-like universe which alternates with an irradiated Eden in the brain of the passionate young.[1]

By a series of movements she is brought down to the country and confronted with facts. She is placed in such a position as to hear Wilfrid categorically deny having ever loved her and at the same time express absolute devotion to the other lady. A scene of tragic blankness ensues between the three. In a wild and blind agony Sandra escapes to London—her only inward cry being, ' My voice! —I have my voice!'[2] And then her voice fails—to her it is like the end. She walks out into the darkness of the winter streets, and in the numbness of her brain hardly knows what happens. When at last she is found by her friend Merthyr Powys, she is not far from collapse, but the crisis is over. Her passion for Wilfrid is behind her; it has gone and left a calm that is more impassable than hatred. Wilfrid sees her

[1] *Sandra Belloni*, chap. xxvi.
[2] *Sandra Belloni*, chap. xxxviii.

again but cannot move her. He has come to realize that she is his real need, but it is too late : she is now and for ever lost to him. He makes her promise, however, that under certain conditions she will not leave England. This for a time keeps her anchored, but when in the unhappiness and uselessness of her present existence she sees the essential futility and baseness of his wish, she boldly breaks the worthless chords. She leaves England for Italy. She has recovered her voice and goes to train it for three years. There has come to her a great longing to help her country, now beginning to show signs of life once more beneath the iron hand of Austria.

Here ends the novel of *Sandra Belloni*. *Vittoria*, which continues her history under very different surroundings, commences after an interval of three years. It is just before the rebellion of 1848. Italy is full of rumours and the uneasy silence that precedes an outbreak. The book opens by a meeting of Italian revolutionaries on the summit of Monte Motterone. Sandra Belloni, now known as the Signorina Vittoria, under which name she is to make her début at Milan, is of the council. The flame of rebellion is to be lit by her by the singing of a revolutionary hymn of patriotism from the boards of La Scala. This is to be the recognized sign for an Italian rising. Here, however, the intricate current of the plot begins to show itself. There is a certain Barto Rizzo who distrusts her, not because she is herself but because she is a woman. He has her spied upon and discovers that she has written to some English friends (they are travelling members of the Pole family) letters warning them not to be in Milan on the night of the 15th. No doubt of her being a traitress remains in his mind. Now the ramifications become too intricate for coherent following in few words. There are endeavours to prevent her singing, but she does not believe in their authority and keeps her inflexible resolve.

Vittoria has come to the full development of her womanhood. Magnificently formed both in appearance and personality, she has crowned the years by a passionate and absorbing patriotism. With the deep and calm conviction of those martyrs who saw beyond the horrid tortures of the flesh the bright and burning vision of their dreams, she carries out her part of the great programme. The night is one of lurid confusion, and in the darkness she is spirited away by friends who would save her from the inevitable imprisonment. But in the moments of this crisis she and Carlo Ammiani, a young man of a noble Milan family, have declared their mutual love. The action of the book moves forward with an incredible sweep of vitality. Vittoria is taken to the Tyrol through adventures that bring out still more clearly the steadfast and deep roots of her character.

The rebellion flashes out and flings across Italy a brand of fire that is the graphic atmosphere and central theme of the romance. And at last when a hundred dramas of death and life have been enacted and Italy once more lies bleeding at the foot of the conqueror, Vittoria marries Carlo Ammiani. But not here does the story end. He is killed by the Austrians in one of these desperate mountain engagements of a lost cause. She hears the news with the terrible calm of one who, in the phrases of Meredith, has passed through the ordeal in the expectation of it. She lives for her child, and if, as we may suppose by the last words of the book, she finally marries Merthyr Powys, it is certain that in him, not only the past but the present, survives in the lives of these two.

Diana of the Crossways is probably the

INSIGHT INTO CHARACTER

cleverest woman drawn by Meredith. By birth Irish, she has the intuitive wit, insight, and fascination of the Irish women. She has too their impulsive, high-strung, and apparently inconsequent nature. But she lives for us. Her rash and astonishing actions are seen to be based upon a fundamental trueness to great ideals of womanhood, and in the false steps she takes there are abundant signs of an inherent nobility and sanity[1] that must raise her in due time to the dower of her inner mind. She is, as Meredith says, 'wind-beaten but ascending'. Our sympathy goes with her, for she has that sort of personality that strikes the deep note of closeness to nature. The problem before us is to explain to some extent the possibility of her character.

Diana is the daughter of a famous Irish wit, Dan Merion, and when only a girl is left an orphan. She has one dear friend, Emma Dunstane. It is with amazement then that Lady Dunstane hears of her engagement to a Mr Warwick, a man of whom she has never heard, and in language that says nothing of love either in words or meaning. The letter contains this sentence, ' Signify your approval, for I have decided that it is

[1] Always with the one exception named hereafter.

the wisest thing a waif can do.'[1] The strangeness of this news is a thousand times increased when Diana brings her husband to her friend. He is a man, cultured, it is true, to some extent, but totally overcome by a sense of narrow order, propriety, and preciseness. Is the explanation to be found in the quoted sentence ?—partly, I think, and partly in the numb reality of becoming engaged and married to one so totally different to all ideals hitherto dominant. I do not know that I make myself clear. Certainly she must have realized with relief the end of anxiety, but she probably would not have become engaged to him had he been very much nearer her own idea of the typical man for her. The marriage continues for two years, and then rumours of dissension begin to spread. Lord Dannisburgh, a statesman holding the highest office, is freely mentioned. Then comes a letter from Diana to Lady Dunstane, saying that Mr Warwick has served her with a process, and that, though the charge is basely false, she cannot stand the publicity and scandal of the courts, and intends to fly either to Ireland or America. It is obvious that such a step would be completely fatal, guilt being assumed

[1] *Diana of the Crossways,* chap. v.

INSIGHT INTO CHARACTER

in the act of flight, and she is persuaded to remain and face out the matter. And though she wins the case, she is not free. Had she only fled, there would at least have been freedom. Here then is another reason which shows that the victory over herself was greater, in as much as it was more clearly perceived, than a mere negation and panic could have allowed. After the separation she lives by writing. She has influential friends and is on the flood of society and literary success.

Then Lord Dannisburgh dies. The relation between them has been the subtle bond of deep affection between an old man, still intellectual, modern, world-wise, and a beautiful woman, unhappy, young, sparkling—an innocent and gallant relationship. At his earnest request she sits an hour by his dead body in the darkness of a silent night. It is now that the Hon. Percy Dacier appears prominently upon the scene. He is the nephew of Lord Dannisburgh and is himself a politician of rising fame, serious, frigid, clever. He has known Diana before and has been gradually falling in love with her, but it is not till his encounter with her in the death-chamber that the reality of his passion springs into conclusiveness. After this there is meeting between them; Diana writes a novel, *The Young Minister of State,* founded obviously on Dacier. Then comes information that Mr Warwick is about to put the law into force to compel his wife to return to him. Dacier entreats her to fly with him and she consents. It is not altogether easy to know what exactly were her feelings for him before the scene in which he sunders the chords of doubt. It is probable that she in no way fully comprehended them and was living in a state of acute blindness to the course of events. But in a moment she awakes to herself, and casts off the old in preparation for the new life. And just before the hour of flight she is summoned to the bedside of Lady Dunstane, who is at the point of death. Thus is she saved again from the precipice. For in calmer moments the calamity of the step is before her and it is definitely dismissed. Mr Warwick dies and there seems now no impediment to the marriage of the two lovers.

One evening he tells her some political news that is of dramatic secrecy for a short period. And here is the one incident of her life that does seem to be impossible of rational explanation. It would seem as if Meredith had imagined or heard of such a real occurrence in such a life and had set himself the task of logically accounting for it, that is to say, accounting for it in such a way as would show its human possibility. Percy has no sooner left, than Diana goes straight to the editor of a great daily paper and sells him the secret. This is the bare fact. The effort of the book is to show that the realization of the act was never before her in its ugly light—that it is in fact another psychological revelation of that incomprehensibility and sudden impulse, which made her marry Mr Warwick, and afterwards suggested flight rather than publicity and lack of freedom, and gave the resolve to fly with Dacier. In these three cases the acts seem strangely like truth, in this case the act seems totally untrue. She is, as we know, a woman of acute perceptions, and though this might be just the pit-fall, as it may have been in the case of her marriage, owing to all the elusiveness of contrast, still, when dealing with actual mundane facts of the moment it is inexplicable that her mind could have been so totally subverted. In the description of her mental state at this crisis Meredith manages to convey a human reality behind the mask, and in this and in the picture of her extraordinary lack of comprehension of the results and gravity of her action, saves the portrait, but only at the price of credence to this part of the history.[1] So great is my admiration for Meredith's knowledge of women, that even now a doubt touches me that he is aware of possibilities in their psychology undreamt of by me, but I cannot but believe that my view must be the general verdict.[2]

Percy Dacier learns from her own lips the story and there and then leaves her for ever. Diana has come to the dark trial of her life. She hopes to die and in the hope learns to live. And then again comes the longing for freedom, which, however, we feel that she knows is only the insecure method of pretending that the future will always be the same as the present. It is clearly seen that she will marry Tom Redworth, and it is this which closes in happiness the story of Diana of the Crossways. She is one of these figures that we see rising to the serenity of an assured outlook ; and great, for being in the act of it, daringly

[1] See also the story of Carinthia Jane's marriage in *The Amazing Marriage* for another example of an inexplicable action.

[2] I am rather inclined to agree with an opinion I have seen somewhere that the smallness of the offence in the eyes of Lady Dunstane and Redworth only tends to increase the unreality of the whole incident.

true to the sincerity of a noble but insecure temperament.

Mr. Chesterton, in one of his extraordinarily brilliant remarks (*Great Thoughts*, October, 1904), speaking of Meredith and others, says, 'They remember this, that however deep, however wild, however baffling and bizarre be the difference between man and man, still it is not a difference between a centaur and a hobgoblin, between a mermaid and a hippogriff, between a kelpie and a dragon.' Here of course is the secret of Meredith's conception and treatment of character. First of all there is the humanity, secondly there is the type, and thirdly there is the individual. We see in his figures a peculiar similarity in dissimilarity. It is the philosophic working through individuality to the basic ground of the type and the common humanity. And strangely enough this is the man who has carried the study of individual personality to a point of fine nuance quite unrivalled. He sees that humanity is one perpetual circle. There is no getting away from its fundamental grip in any intricate psychological examination of a phase. Where the track seems dimmest in strange depths of individualism we meet its full tide, and at last it will dawn upon us that we have been travelling with it all the time. In fact we end much where we started as far as abstract truth goes, though actually we have gained experience for the matters of this world.

There are great standpoints from which Meredith surveys life. There is the standpoint of the comic spirit, from which everything is observed with a still, unerring quietness. Its inward eye seeks out the sentimentalism, the egoism, the shams of our existence. It lays them bare and holds upon them a dissection not less minute than philosophic. The comic spirit is not merely a weapon of scourging—it holds the just balance of sanity and mental alertness, and is serenely pleased as long as they are not tampered with.

And there is the standpoint of nature, from which is seen the elemental philosophy of existence. From it he notes man's defective realization of nature's beneficence, and constantly urges a closer and more harmonious intercourse with her.

And there is the standpoint of humanity from which our common brotherhood is recognized. From it he sees the joy and the tragedy of life; he sees death and life and the dark night of tormented souls and the immortality of love; he sees crime, ideals, hope, infamy, but he sees them all philosophically, for they are all human. The very fact of having such penetrating insight to character has, I think, kept from him the complete spirit of brotherhood. If I may say so, Meredith is too intellectual to have absolute sympathy with all humanity. I remarked just above, that he sees crime, ideals, hope, infamy all philosophically because they are all human, but if I had been writing the same thing of Walt Whitman, I should have used the word 'tenderly' instead of 'philosophically'. That is just the difference between the two men—Meredith marvellous in detail and marvellous also in philosophic perception of abstract character and universal trends of character, Whitman hazy and heedless of detail and set philosophic thought, but greatly daring in his soul, to cast from him everything but the ideal spark that is in humanity, that spark that lurks no less in the murderer than the saint. It is in this quality alone then (and doubtless it is largely a quality of temperament), in which Meredith fails to reach the most profound and exact idea of character.

CHAPTER VII

On Tragedy

WE are now to deal with tragedy, the tragic spirit and the relative power of their tragic and just presentation. It is true that Meredith's idea of comedy includes tragedy, in the sense that comedy is the impersonal view on all human affairs. Tragedy can be filled with comedy; that is to say, it can be the outcome of a sequence, in the full scourge of the comic spirit. The elements of such tragedy are in fact essentially comic, essentially apparent to the keen and wise vision of the comic writer.

The novelist has to deal with two main themes of tragedy—the innate tragedy of every life, the slow flame of which is so easily aroused, and the sudden tragedy of terrible and unexpected events, equally inherent and innate. The novelist is not the least of psychologists. He is a worker in the dark pit of our foundations, and of these tragedy is one. The tragedy of souls, in all their million intricate windings and sub-conscious reasonings, are the pawns of his subtle and earnest handling.

Once more it cannot be too strongly insisted that here again art is the true correlative of imaginative grasp. James Thomson, the poet and critic, writing of Meredith many years ago, said 'he always rises with his theme, growing more strenuous, more self-contained, more magistral, as the demands on his thoughts and imagination increase'.[1] These are very remarkable words because they hold the essence of the eternal artistic presentation of tragedy, and the meaning of that inevitableness which has lain at the root of it from the time of the Greeks and long before. For however finely we may conceive the elements of the tragedy of a soul, its threads are nevertheless discernible, leading with ever-rising clearness of distinction, ever-increasing sharpness of outline, to the final catastrophy. The seeds of such tragedy are small, but they are like fate. And how true are Thomson's words, when we consider what should be the artistic handling of sudden tragedy. Surely here is demanded that simple intensity of language and thought, mounting, with a

[1] *Essays and Phantasies*, p. 294.

feeling of huge forces held in reserve, as the imagination deepens upon the scene. Everything calls for power, simplicity, indeed majestic acceptance of man's limits.

Then again, the novelist has to realize that tragedy is intensely personal, that to grasp it he needs great power of imagination and sympathy—a thing quite apart from the philosophical survey of the comic spirit. Meredith's profound greatness lies in his double grasp of the subject. The comic spirit has saved him from sentimentality, the human understanding from too cold a basis of logic. They have together given him that insight which sees the tragedy of tragedy, but sees it from the hill of the optimist. For tragedy is really one of philosophy's handmaidens, one of the human meanings of abstract and universal ideas. Meredith is as usual true to the reasonable view of existence. Like the idea of absolute good, we may say there is such a thing as absolute tragedy — a philosophic thought on a thing that exists only in theory. In life and even in our actual theories on life we know that tragedy, like all impersonal words, is a scale of gradations seen through a thousand facets of fact and imagination.

ON TRAGEDY

The purely tragic is an unknown quantity and is treated as such by Meredith. There are tragedies of fate, tragedies of man—mixed, blending, flowing in winding channels that cross and re-cross till beyond the limits of our grasp. Meredith has certainly given us several figures that are tragic almost in that concentrated, fateful way of the old Greeks. Of such figures, perhaps Barto Rizzo's wife in *Vittoria* is the most tragic. She is the essence of that spirit of tragedy, sprung from fate and bounded only by time. The whole conception of her character is of the inherent tragedy of the re-action of personality and environment. She lives in a mist, blindly groping with the aid of the smouldering fires of primary senses to knowledge of herself. Her personality shows that simple concentration of intensity which is the true tragic touch. Her life must have been to her a kind of mysterious almost impersonal dream—Barto Rizzo himself a stranger gleam in it. Then her meeting with Rinaldo Guidascarpi. It is her awakening to the personality of life. She rouses slowly to know herself in the dim way in which wild animals seem to catch at meanings. She is so tragic, because she is so elemental, therefore so cosmic and convincing. Her love for him is that primary love which is beyond explanation or words : it is her life. What tremendous power of presentiment and tragic insight to the deep workings of the terrible, slumbrous forces of her nature, there is in the description of her letting Rinaldo and Wilfrid Pole escape from Barto's house—

He said to Wilfrid in her presence, ' Swear that you will reveal nothing of this house.'
Wilfrid spiritedly pronounced his gladdest oath.
' It is dark in the streets,' Rinaldo addressed the woman. ' Lead us out, for the hour has come when I must go.'
She clutched her hands below her bosom to stop its great heaving, and stood as one smitten by the sudden hearing of her sentence. The sight was pitiful, for her face scarcely changed ; the anguish was expressionless. Rinaldo pointed sternly to the door.
' Stay,' Wilfrid interposed. ' That wretch may be in the house, and will kill her.'
' She is not thinking of herself,' said Rinaldo.
' But, stay,' Wilfrid repeated. The woman's way of taking breath shocked and enfeebled him.
Rinaldo threw the door open.
' Must you ? must you ? ' her voice broke.
' Waste no words.'
' You have not seen a priest.'
' I go to him.'
' You die.'
' What is death to me ? Be dumb, that I may think well of you till my last moment.'
' What is death to me ? Be dumb ! '
She had spoken with her eyes fixed on his couch. It was the figure of one upon the scaffold, knitting her frame to hold up a strangled heart.

'What is death to me? Be dumb!' she echoed him many times on the rise and fall of her breathing, and turned to get him in her eyes. 'Be dumb! be dumb!' She threw her arms wide out, and pressed his temples and kissed him.[1]

Their talk seems to come to her like an echo of half-caught meanings. There is no acting about her, only the dumb intensity of despair and death. This is great writing.

Built in somewhat the same tragic mould are the brothers Guidascarpi.[2] Though men of distinguished rank and intelligence, they are shrouded by the dark story of their sister's death, and their revenge. They are fanatics, and such are always tragic. These three figures seem in a way the most tragically imagined in his books; that is to say, they seem the most purely tragic in the fundamental essence of their characters. Though we see clearly enough the outward influences that were at work to ruin them, we feel that they carried in them the touch of fate.

Mrs Victor Radnor, in *One of our Conquerors*, is only less tragic. We certainly do not imagine her as primarily a tragic figure. The human influence on her life is paramount, and it is easy to see that she could have been

[1] *Vittoria*, chap. xxix.   [2] *Vittoria*.

moulded to something very different. But there is this thing noticeable about her. Once she has taken the decisive step of her life, immediately she is in the grip of the powers of tragic fate. In such a character it is the only imaginable result, for to begin with she must have been one of the questioning women, in whom there are always strong elements of tragedy that sleep or wake as the currents of their lives go. It is this element which gives us a certain half-tragedy in the lives of Diana Warwick,[1] Rhoda Fleming,[2] Rosamond Culling,[3] Sandra Belloni,[4] and numerous others. There is something terrible in her double knowledge of her powerlessness. She feels that she is dying and she feels that fate has found her. Her inability to speak to Victor or Nesta and her estrangement from them almost because of her love for them is part of her trial. The meaning of her words, ' At peace when the night is over ', is shown with that restraint and power which is the true medium for such pent up emotions.

The box-door opened, Dartrey came in. He took

---

[1] *Diana of the Crossways.*
[2] *Rhoda Fleming.*   [3] *Beauchamp's Career.*
[4] *Sandra Belloni* and *Vittoria.*

ON TRAGEDY

her hand. She stood up to his look. He said to Matilda Pridden : ' Come with us ; she will need you.'
  ' Speak it,' said Nesta.
  He said to the other : ' She has courage.'
  ' I could trust to her,' Matilda Pridden replied.
  Nesta read his eyes. ' Mother ? '
  His answer was in the pressure.
  ' Ill ? '
  ' No longer.'
  ' Oh ! Dartrey.'
  Matilda Pridden caught her fast.
  ' I can walk, dear,' Nesta said.
  Dartrey mentioned her father.
  She understood. ' I am thinking of him.'
  The words of her mother : ' At peace when the night is over ' rang. Along the gassy passages of the back of the theatre, the sound coming from an applausive audience was as much a thunder as rage would have been. It was as void of human meaning as a sea.[1]

Consider again such a character as the shadowy Chloe in *The Tale of Chloe*—woman who has been loved and still loves. She too is of that deeply tragic cast which wears a mask and dies inwardly. Her actual death was truly her second death. Think also of Clare Forey in *Richard Feverel*. She also is the outwardly calm and inwardly shrieking victim of circumstance. Juliana Bonner in *Evan Harrington* is another of these women dead to hope, but fighting still her tragic fate. We feel that for these three there is peace

---

[1] *One of our Conquerors*, chap. xli.

in the grave. As Meredith finely says of the death of Juliana Bonner—

> Caroline promised to obey, and coming to Juliana to mark her looks, observed a faint pleased smile dying away, and had her hand gently squeezed. Juliana's conscience had preceded her contentedly to its last sleep; and she, beneath that round of light on the ceiling, drew on her counted breaths in peace till dawn.[1]

Rhoda Fleming is a tragic story. It is the especially bitter one of the tragedy of a betrayed woman. Dahlia Fleming is far more of a martyr than of a sinning woman, and one could almost say to her as Victor Hugo makes Jean Valjean say to Fantine... 'je vous le déclare dès à présent... vous n'avez jamais cessé d'être vertueuse et sainte devant Dieu. Oh! pauvre femme!'[2] Still she is the victim and even the scapegoat, and such is a common enough story in our present civilization. These are strange words, in which her soul is described as looking through her eyes, for one moment

> Once more the inexplicable frozen look struck over him from her opened eyes, as if one of the minutes of Time had yawned to show him its deep, mute, tragic abyss, and was extinguished.[3]

and her last words are tragic with her

---

[1] *Evan Harrington*, chap. xlii.
[2] *Les Misérables*, book 5, chap. xiii.
[3] *Rhoda Fleming*, chap. xxx.

ON TRAGEDY

awakened realization of the lot of woman in this world—

> Almost her last words to him, spoken calmly, but with the quaver of breath resembling sobs, were : ' Help poor girls.' [1]

In *Modern Love* also the whole conception is tragic. It is the tragedy of the dead love of a young married couple, tinged with doubt, remorse, and pangs of jealousy. The poem is great, for the language is very magnificent, and rises to heights of lyrical splendour not unsuited to the tragic memories of the past. This verse of comparison between now and then is surely the essence of the word ' regret '.

> In our old shipwrecked days there was an hour,
> When in the firelight steadily aglow,
> Joined slackly, we beheld the red chasm grow
> Among the clicking coals. Our library bower
> That ever was left to us : and hushed we sat
> As lovers to whom Time is whispering.
> From sudden-opened doors we heard them sing :
> The nodding elders mixed good wine with chat.
> Well knew we that Life's greatest treasure lay
> With us, and of it was our talk. ' Ah, yes ! Love dies ! ' I said : I never thought it less.
> She yearned to me that sentence to unsay.
> Then when the fire domed blackening, I found
> Her cheek was salt against my kiss, and swift
> Up the sharp scale of sobs her breast did lift :—
> Now am I haunted by that taste ! that sound ! [2]

---

[1] *Rhoda Fleming*, chap. xlviii.
[2] Stanza xvi.

As has already been said, tragedy, as indeed all the great subjects, lends itself in Meredith's hands to subtle shades of treatment. He has seen in his universality and depth of perception the gradations of which we are built and the true meaning of personality. Take for instance the three leading figures in *The Ordeal of Richard Feverel*—Sir Austin, Richard, Lucy. They are all of them tragic, but with such differences, that three words instead of one might comprehend them. Sir Austin's is the tragedy of diseased egoism and morbid introspection. We are told how they came to full life through his betrayal by the wife and friend he had trusted so completely. But the more we consider him, the more we shall see that no fully healthy mind could have developed so far along such lines even in the bitterest circumstances. Study of him will show that he had born in him the devil of blindness. Sir Austin is especially tragic, for he is a most lonely figure and in all ways a remarkable one.

Richard Feverel is finely imagined as differing from his father greatly, but rather in the trend of his imagination than in the qualities of his brain. Of course it is easy to take up a false position in this kind of criticism where any colouring will seem to fit the facts together, but it seems to me that we can trace in Richard's fall the same causes which ruined Sir Austin's life. They were both high-minded men who had ideals : Sir Austin had the ideal of friendship, Richard the ideal of reformation. One over-rated his knowledge, the other his power—and they are much the same thing. They each fell from a height and for each the effect was revolutionary. Here we begin to see the difference of their characters. Richard had the introspection of his father, but he had not nearly such a full share of blind egoism. Nothing could have opened Sir Austin's eyes —the final catastrophe did not—but Richard had his awakening in the night-storm in the forest. He is far more human than Sir Austin as we see him, and probably more human than Sir Austin ever was. One does not easily imagine Sir Austin having tragic scenes with his wife—he has too much of the egoist's easily-wounded self-pride, but we remember Richard's interview with Lucy—

'Lucy. Do you know why I came to you to-night ? '
She moved her lips repeating his words.
'Lucy. Have you guessed why I did not come before ? '

Her head shook widened eyes.

'Lucy. I did not come because I was not worthy of my wife! Do you understand?'

'Darling,' she faltered plaintively, and hung crouching under him, 'what have I done to make you angry with me?'

'O beloved!' he cried, the tears bursting out of his eyes. 'O beloved!' was all he could say, kissing her hands passionately.

She waited, reassured, but in terror.

'Lucy. I stayed away from you—I could not come to you, because . . . I dared not come to you, my wife, my beloved! I could not come because I was a coward; because—hear me—this was the reason: I have broken my marriage oath.'

Again her lips moved. She caught at a dim fleshless meaning in them. 'But you love me? Richard! My husband! you love me?'

'Yes. I have never loved, I never shall love, woman but you.'

'Darling! Kiss me.'

'Have you understood what I have told you?'

'Kiss me,' she said.

He did not join lips. 'I have come to you to-night to ask your forgiveness.'

Her answer was: 'Kiss me.'

'Can you forgive a man so base?'

'But you love me, Richard?'

'Yes: that I can say before God. I love you, and I have betrayed you, and am unworthy of you—not worthy to touch your hand, to kneel at your feet, to breathe the same air with you.'

Her eyes shone brilliantly. 'You love me! you love me, darling!' And as one who has sailed through dark fears into daylight, she said: 'My husband! my darling! you will never leave me? We never shall be parted again?'[1]

---

[1] *The Ordeal of Richard Feverel*, chap. xliv.

Even when he falls, it is with the tragic intensity of the humanist. His whole upbringing and some basic quality of imaginative fire gave him a nobler grip of life than his father had. He was wrecked by Sir Austin's system, but he would not have been wrecked had he not been the child of his father, and he would not have come to his regeneration had he not been more than the child of his father.

Lucy has a far less complicated character than either of the other two, and the tragedy of her life is the simple tragedy of circumstance. Naturally, there is nothing tragic about her—she is the pawn of events. Still she suffers tragically and dies in darkness.

> 'She died five days after she had been removed. The shock had utterly deranged her. I was with her. She died very quietly, breathing her last breath without pain, asking for no one—a death I should like to die.
>
> 'Her cries at one time were dreadfully loud. She screamed that she was "drowning in fire" and that her husband would not come to her to save her. We deadened the sound as much as we could, but it was impossible to prevent Richard from hearing. He knew her voice, and it produced an effect like fever on him. Whenever she called he answered. You could not hear them without weeping.'[1]

Again, there are figures in these novels that

[1] *The Ordeal of Richard Feverel*, chap. xlv.

seem tragic through their own wilfulness or eccentricity. They are kind of tragic comedians, as Meredith himself might call them. Alvan[1] is one, Lord Fleetwood[2] is one, Lord Ormont[3] is one, Sir Willoughby Patterne[4] is one, Richmond Roy[5] is one. None of these men are really sane, and their views of life are distorted—a thing which leads to disaster. The victims of sentimentality may also be called tragic—Wilfrid Pole[6] verges on it, Sir Purcell Barret[7] dies by his own hand. These are the tragedies of bitterness, such as Colney Durance,[8] and the tragedies of overconfidence, such as Victor Radnor.[9]

Nevil Beauchamp, like Lucy Desborough, is not innately a tragic figure, and his tragic death is somehow a natural climax to this life of surprises. His is such a beautifully imagined portrait that we feel the fitness of his last act almost more than its fatal results. It seems as though it were the completion of his character and not the completion of his life. Meredith's writing here is grandly suited to the thrilling and great story of his death.

[1] *The Tragic Comedians.*   [2] *The Amazing Marriage.*
[3] *Lord Ormont and His Aminta.*   [4] *The Egoist.*
[5] *The Adventures of Harry Richmond.*   [6,7] *Sandra Belloni.*
[8,9] *One of our Conquerors.*

ON TRAGEDY

How simple, how compressed, how full of the quiet of deep power are the ringing sentences. It is perhaps the noblest piece of tragic writing in the whole series of his books. Though long, it is right that it should be given in full—

This is no time to tell of weeping. The dry chronicle is fittest. Hard on nine o'clock in the December darkness, the night being still and clear, Jenny's babe was at her breast, and her ears were awake for the return of her husband. A man rang at the door of the house, and asked to see Dr Shrapnel. This man was Killick, the Radical Sam of politics. He said to the doctor : ' I'm going to hit you sharp, sir : I've had it myself : please put on your hat and come out with me, and close the door. They mustn't hear inside. And here's a fly, I knew you'd be off for the finding of the body. Commander Beauchamp's drowned.'

Dr Shrapnel drove round by the shore of the broad water past a great hospital and ruined abbey to Otley village. Killick had lifted him into the conveyance and he lifted him out. Dr Shrapnel had not spoken a word. Lights were flaring on the river, illuminating the small craft sombrely. Men, women, and children crowded the hard and landing places, the marshy banks and the decks of colliers and trawlers. Neither Killick nor Dr Shrapnel questioned them. The lights were torches and lanterns ; the occupation of the boats moving in couples was the dragging for the dead.

' O God, let's find his body,' a woman called out.

' Just a word ; is it Commander Beauchamp ? ' Killick said to her.

She was scarcely aware of a question. ' Here, this one,' she said, and plucked a little boy of eight by the hand close against her side, and shook him roughly and kissed him.

An old man volunteered information. 'That's the boy. That boy was in his father's boat out there, with two of his brothers, larking; and he and another older than him fell overboard; and just then Commander Beauchamp was rowing by, and I saw him from off here, where I stood, jump up and dive, and he swam to his boat with one of them and got him in safe: that boy: and he dived again after the other, and was down a long time. Either he burst a vessel or he got cramp, for he'd been rowing himself from the schooner grounded down at the river mouth, and must have been hot when he jumped in, either way, he fetched the second up and sank with him. Down he went.'

A fisherman said to Killick: 'Do you hear that voice thundering? That's the great Lord Romfrey. He's been directing the dragging since five o' the evening, and will till he drops or drowns, or up comes the body.'

'O God, let's find the body!' the woman with the little boy called out.

A torch lit up Lord Romfrey's face as he stepped ashore.

'The flood has played us a trick,' he said. 'We want more drags, or with the next ebb the body may be lost for days in this infernal water.'

The mother of the rescued boy sobbed, 'Oh, my lord, my lord!'

The earl caught sight of Dr Shrapnel and went to him.

'My wife has gone down to Mrs Beauchamp,' he said. 'She will bring her and the baby to Mount Laurels. The child will have to be hand-fed. I take you with me. You must not be alone.'

He put his arm within the arm of the heavily-breathing man whom he had once flung to the ground, to support him.

'My lord! my lord!' sobbed the woman, and dropped on her knees.

'What is this?' the earl said, drawing his hand away from the woman's clutch at it.

'She's the mother, my lord,' several explained to him.
'Mother of what?'
'My boy,' the woman cried, and dragged the urchin to Lord Romfrey's feet, cleaning her boy's face with her apron.
'It's the boy Commander Beauchamp drowned to save,' said a man.
All the lights of the ring were turned on the head of the boy. Dr Shrapnel's eyes and Lord Romfrey's fell on the abashed little creature. The boy struck out both arms to get his fists against his eyelids.
This is what we have in exchange for Beauchamp!
It was not uttered, but it was visible in the blank stare at one another of the two men who loved Beauchamp, after they had examined the insignificant bit of mudbank life remaining in this world in the place of him.[1]

This is the language of someone with a giant's grasp of the fateful moments of our lives. Meredith's tragic writing has that thrill which is true.

Of the novels, it is perhaps safe to say that four only are conceived as tragedies in the fuller meaning of the word—*The Ordeal of Richard Feverel, Rhoda Fleming, The Tragic Comedians,* and *One of our Conquerors* : to these might be added *The Tale of Chloe.* In them the plot is subservient to a tragic finale and we are shown all the webs and threads of fateful happenings. Heavy presentiment hangs over them and we feel a

[1] *Beauchamp's Career,* chap. lvi.

certain inexorable grasp narrowing everything to one channel. There is certainly in the tragic a unanimity of action and a concentration on the end which is probably the cause of the ancient idea of fate in it. Meredith has seen plainly how inevitably results spring from actions and how inevitably actions hang on one another.

Now we have examined shortly some of the typical tragic figures of Meredith's creation, but in doing so there is of course the danger of our losing sight of what really tragedy and the tragic idea mean to such a writer. Too minute a view misses the perspective, which is the spirit, of the thing.

To George Meredith then what actually is tragedy and the significance of the tragic? To answer that question it is necessary to realize the power of fate over man and of man over himself. Meredith sees tragedy as a mixture of the innate and the avoidable. It is deep calling to deep. It is the unmasking of man's mortality and the understanding of the pains of existence. It is a philosophical reminder of unknown laws and of infinite workings. Tragedy to him is a stern stimulus to thought. Its gloomy depths of volcanic calm lead on the imagination to pierce beyond the face of its heaving surface. Tragedy is the storehouse of wronged nature whose everlasting law calls for just measure and requital. There is an eye that can pierce beyond it to imagine the real and final peace of nature. The optimist sees in tragedy something deep, but not so deep as his optimism. Meredith, the optimist, has known those laws, of which tragedy is but one of the methods of fulfilment. All the harmonies of nature, whose million voices echo into one deep note, are like the waves, whose countless breakings become the murmur of the soundless sea. Tragedy then appears to Meredith a lesson of philosophy and not a lesson of despairing anguish. I would refer any one who doubts this to his poem *A Faith on Trial*, where poignant grief finds rest in the haven of philosophy. Knowledge is to give us the key of tragedy and then will be seen those fuller meanings of nature, whose workings are now but dimly understood.

CHAPTER VIII

On Death

A MAN's real views on death more accurately describe his real views on life than anything else. This is not the paradox it might appear to be. For then at last must fade from him all but the essential things. His reading of death's riddle defines for him the meaning of life. In a moment, brought within himself to face this last question, he unconsciously draws back into the foundations that are eternal. It is then he sees that he has been building all the phantasy of his imagination upon a certain basis, to him indestructible, and sees fully (for the first time in all probability) what really that basis is. For assumptions gain weight with the years, and are only viewed in their bare nakedness when the sudden shock opens, for one instant, the eyes of the blind assumer.

And so, if it were for this reason alone, I think that much would be gained by seeing what Meredith's views on death are. It is true enough that we have had to touch on this at several points, but so far we have not attempted any real definition. We have observed indeed that his philosophy of life and nature embraces in its scheme of optimism and progress the fact of death, but we have observed it only in a wide and what may be called impersonal way. These thoughts woven of life that run through his works in continuous threads of distinct and individual ideas are based upon the immortality of life itself. My purpose here is rather to consider what are his emotions when the actual physical fact of death has to be faced. A man who can watch the death of some one dear to him, and still have before him the calm and clear scheme of eternal peace, is a man whose optimism is based on something as strong as death itself. The man whose sanity rises over such wild and bitter grief is one whose philosophy is not merely literary and academic. It is a philosophy of life founded upon the deepest facts of life, and tried in the furnace of actuality.

But it is not only for this reason that I wish to make this examination. Than death there are few subjects more inherently capable of the most noble artistic treatment. Nothing so floods the mind with majestic and solemn imagery and fires the imagination with tremendous conjecture. We seem brought to the footstool of one of the gods of cosmos and surrounded by a kind of subtle atmosphere that betokens his very presence. There is a something in death in the highest degree thoughtful and elemental. We know very well that it has inspired many of the greatest triumphs of art, and we can see that it is the factor in a thousand dramatic and thrilling episodes. And therefore I think that the treatment of death by an author is a vital test of the width and power of his grasp.

Thus there are two main positions (which infallibly rest on one another) from which we are to judge Meredith's ideas of death—the philosophic position and the artistic position. And remember that the novelist has to face death as a very real and tangible thing. He may, as in the case of Meredith, include it in the broad basis of his philosophy, but over and above that, he has to meet it as a thing palpably affecting the reality of his creations He has to realize the meaning of death, not only to himself in the abstract, but to his characters in the personal. He has to grasp, as a lightning-flash, the bewildering and incalculable thoughts that actual death brings forth, and see how vital is its influence in the affairs of life. Meredith's own views of death lean strongly towards an optimism not founded on any hope of personal immortality. Being a process in the evolution of life, it cannot be unkind, even though to the individual it should spell extinction. He believes in the immortality of action, and the immortality of the spark of existence. In fact, though reverently agnostic towards the unknowable, he holds a more definite attitude of doubt to the question of the survival of personality, than that of the purely colourless agnostic.

By the very use of the word infinity we imagine a thing on an equal level of importance called finity, but surely finity is only possible in infinity. People talk about infinity as if it were a thing that would start at some time in the future, but of course we are in infinity now, and there was no beginning to it and there can be no end. Death cannot claim us nor the shades of night have victory over us. The elements that form us are immortal and time is the one vision of dreamless eternity. All around us is phantasma and illusion. Nothing exists but as the creation of our own minds, and at last the uneasy spirit of the ego will itself slumber again. We shall yield our spirits into the great soul of all things and our lives into the calm of perpetual night. O sleep, into whose silence, dreams strange and beautiful as life come only to pass away, keep us from the darkness of sensation; let us drink once of thee and rest indeed for ever. Death merges us in the ceaseless flux of creation. Personality may not survive, but the essence of life cannot be destroyed. Our comprehension of years means nothing in the light of ages and all metaphysics return upon themselves. Death takes us out of the backwater of life and flings us once again into that awful tide that sets in an eternal sea.

There are certain schools that write about death with a morbid tendency to detail belonging more to the ghoul than to the artist. At one time sentimental platitudes defined the range of expression about it, at another a hideous pondering on corruption. Such thoughts are of no value and indeed they come from vapid or unwholesome brains. Really great men like Whitman and Meredith have naturally realized the necessity and kindness of death. They do not talk about life and death as if they had no relation to one another, but as if they were naturally the true continuation of each other. Were I writing a book about Walt Whitman, I could give superb examples of my meaning in such poems as *Whispers of Heavenly Death, Out of the Cradle endlessly Rocking*, and so forth, but we can clearly perceive a not dissimilar though perhaps less obvious spirit, in the writings of Meredith. Take this quotation from *One of our Conquerors*—

Death among us proves us to be still not so far from the Nature saying at every avenue to the mind ; *Earth makes all sweet*.[1]

and this one from *Ode to the Spirit of Earth in Autumn*—

> And O, green bounteous Earth !
> Bacchante Mother ! stern to those
> Who live not in thy heart of mirth ;
> Death shall I shrink from, loving thee ?
> Into the breast that gives the rose
>   Shall I with shuddering fall ?

That is the way that Meredith's philosophy looks on death. If there is one thing strongly repugnant to him, it is the morbid or the sentimental. Both his philosophy and his manhood revolt against any such emotions.

[1] Chap. xlii.

Browning in such poems as *Prospice* and the *Epilogue* to *Asolando* would represent his manly view of it, and Meredith himself in his *The Question Whither*, his philosophical view.

But he has of course a profoundly dramatic sense of the shock and disaster of death. In all lives the philosophic is suddenly confronted with the actual in a way that is overwhelming. Lucy's death in *Richard Feverel*, Beauchamp's death in *Beauchamp's Career*, Mrs Victor Radnor's death in *One of our Conquerors*, are leaves from a tragic Diary. The death chamber of Lord Dannisburgh in *Diana of the Crossways* arouses in the two watchers in it, thoughts that inevitably follow in the train of death—

> Alternately in his mind Death had vaster meanings and doubtfuller; Life cowered under the shadow or outshone it.[1]

> 'Death is natural,' he said.
> 'It is natural to the aged. When they die honoured . . .' She looked where the dead man lay. 'To sit beside the young, cut off from their dear opening life! . . .' A little shudder swept over her. 'Oh! that!'[2]

They are the everlasting questions, beating upon the hopeless doors of night. For in these moments all the problems of destiny

---

[1,2] *Diana of the Crossways*, chap. xx.

and fate whirl round us in frightful complexity of doubt. Nowhere is light. Meredith has fought out this battle for himself in *A Faith on Trial,* which should be read for a true understanding of his philosophy.

The word artistic has come to have a meaning that makes its use in connection with a word like death appear false. But nevertheless the subject is one that requires the finest artistic handling. The grandeur and sadness and triumph of death need moving and great language; the thoughts that spring from it, the wings of eloquence and the sword of prophecy.

You will perhaps remember how Alvan, in *The Tragic Comedians,* crossed and re-crossed in his walk a dead and sombre tree that seemed to strike a chill into his very heart.[1] That is one aspect of the spirit of death. For the cold dews gather round its brow and misty silence creeps before it. Grief in its intensest moments is dumb, and sorrow is the child of loneliness.

Some mid-Victorian writers were in the habit of dwelling with sickly insistence upon death-scenes and of presenting us in consequence with elaborate records of dissolutions.

[1] Chap. vii.

They were really extremely depressing, for they were neither life-like nor tragic, but merely sentimental and mawkish. Such descriptions showed little knowledge of life and no knowledge of art. Meredith has entirely outsoared this phase. If there is a scene of death to be recorded, he records it in few sentences, but with a solemn comprehension of the great reality. At such times a plethora of words obscures the atmosphere and dims the thought. Nowhere has he lingered on last words or lovingly pondered on dying respirations. For that side of death that is extinction can only bring temporary despair to the philosopher, viewing it in the light of abstraction. The night may be full of weeping, but joy cometh in the morning. To Meredith death is that sleep that renews the flame of life. It is only another aspect of the immense cycle of change and advance. Love conquers the fear of death, which perhaps may mean that the spirit of humanity, battling forward for ever, will in time open all our eyes to a wider scheme of existence. As Whitman says in his exalted *Reconciliation*—

> Word over all, beautiful as the sky,
> Beautiful that war and all its deeds of carnage must in time be utterly lost,

> That the hands of the Sisters Death and Night
> incessantly softly wash again and ever again
> this soiled world.

Language could not express more nobly this great idea.

And again, death holds the keys of memory. Its presence reverses the order of expectancy. For while there is life we look forward, but when there is death we look back. As over some sleeping city a flash of lightning darts a sudden and metallic gleam, throwing into relief of unspeakable brightness a million points of detail and a thousand signs of energy, and instantly, before we have quite taken in the picture, sinks back into the night, leaving behind it a darkness as gloomy and impenetrable as before, so memory flings its gleams upon the forests of the past. It is death that keeps the light steadfast. Step by step we follow in the path of recollection, and inch by inch we unfold its silent roll. Now no longer is there distraction in a moving picture. A definite period has to be grasped and lived over once again. The vagueness of an unfinished picture gives place to the clear-cut lines of a finished one. There is in such thoughts a passion of regret, but not of despair. As Meredith says so grandly in *Modern Love*—

> Then, as midnight makes
> Her giant heart of Memory and Tears
> Drink the pale drug of silence, and so beat
> Sleep's heavy measure. .[1]

and makes us feel the impassive records of memory. The storm clouds will pass away and a calm sunset, bathing as in rays of coming night, settle with quietness upon the soul. Throughout Meredith's work there is a remarkable dwelling on what might be called ' The memory of the past ', for not only is there in him the spirit of contemplation, but born of that, a powerful philosophy of experience.

And so death at the last means little more to him than inevitable and beautiful rest and renewal. Unable to see beyond it, he can see that it at least is human and what had to be. He does not put it out of his true schemes of progress, but feels that it not only has to be reckoned in them, but that it is good that it should be; not only accepts it because it is certain; but because it is right that it should be certain. The chants of death are in the deepest sense the chants of life, and the hymns of death, hymns of triumph.

[1] Stanza i.

ON DEATH

Many must have gone to the Morgue from curiosity who came away thoughtful. Even in the horrible faces of the murdered and the drowned there was still apparent a solemn and majestic look, like the unwearied gaze of the sphinx. It was not merely the contrast between their intense unspeculative stillness and the activity of the street that would strike the onlookers, but a strange sense that they had already solved a question which is the question of life and death and had entered upon that trance which must in due time engulf us all in irretrievable oblivion. The swollen and distorted faces of those fished with nets out of the Seine, the torn and frightful faces of those killed in ghastly incidents and dark deeds, the calm, pale faces of those who died suddenly without warning, the hopeless face of the suicide, the violent and malformed face of the lunatic, and the frightened faces of little children, all bore upon them a look which blotted out the meanness of the surroundings and the sensible expressions of death, and which was more noble and ethereal than the looks of living people. It was such as we can imagine those to wear who see at last the meaning of all, and realize that at length they have passed through the gates of the night into that place, where (in the beautiful imagery of the New Testament) all tears shall be wiped from their eyes, and sighing and weeping shall be no more. Thoughts like these have inspired Meredith's ideas on death and the meaning of death.

But surely we get his final views on actual knowledge in those impressive words that close the story of *Modern Love*—

> Ah, what a dusty answer gets the soul
> When hot for certainties in this our life!—
> In tragic hints here see what evermore
> Moves dark as yonder midnight ocean's force,
> Thundering like ramping hosts of warrior horse,
> To throw that faint thin line upon the shore![1]

It is his admission that after all is said and done, we know no more about life than what we started out with; that all the arguments and movements we can follow up lead only to the 'faint thin line' of supposition.

[1] Stanza 1.

CHAPTER IX

On Love

EVERYTHING that is included in the usual and intense meaning of the word love, that word which means all human joy in glimpses of an eternal something, has been the aim and the pinnacle of art through ages. Universally it is the final justification and splendour of life. Every one has been writing about it since literature began and on it have been played such countless notes, that it has come to be the one direct emotion on which we can compare anyone with everyone. And so for two reasons it is valuable to the expounder and the critic. Firstly, because it is such an immense and boundless influence, and secondly because it is such a unique background to the critical faculty. A writer who writes with power and imagination on love, and whose artistic handling seems equal to our realization of it, must surely be a great writer. We see him entering into that strange emotion, and if he can take us with him, we know that he has the touch of mastery. For the emotion is one so inexplicable and personal that we must to some extent cast from us the coldness of the artist and grasp instead the essence of the idea, to fully know the truth and beauty of the picture. We must, in fact, again conjure up the thoughts of the lover, to enter that region. For the lover alone knows the symbols that stand for life and eternity; he alone feels that love is equal to the dreams of an ideal. An unknown light has cast upon time a new significance and upon the earth a band of fire; the thrill of his heart has awakened a thrill that is in all things.

And it is mainly for such a reason that I wish to examine George Meredith's conception and treatment of love, for by doing so we shall see how great a writer he really is. To him love is the giant awakener, it is what makes us grasp the reality of ourselves and of existence. It is a passion which purifies itself through a knowledge of its own inspiration. As he says—

Is it any waste of time to write of love? The trials of life are in it, but in a narrow ring and a fierier. You may learn to know yourself through love, as you do after years of life, whether you are fit to lift them that are about you, or whether you are but a cheat, and a load on the backs of your fellows. The impure perishes, the inefficient languishes, the moderate comes to its autumn of decay—these are of the kinds which aim at satisfaction to die of it soon or late. The love that survives has strangled craving; it lives because it lives to nourish and succour like the heavens.[1]

and it is a fine thought. For to him it is the message of man's grandest unselfishness and of the deepest emotions possible to us. Meredith understands what love is, a mixture of every pain and every joy, a well of despair and triumph, of agony and gladness, of selfishness, of self-immolation. It is a remarkable poem in which he voices the craving for love, even through knowledge of its mortality—

> Ask, is Love divine,
> Voices all are, ay.
> Question for the sign,
> There's a common sigh.
> Would we through our years,
> Love forego,
> Quit of scars and tears?
> Ah, but no, no, no![2]

The sense of its embodied fleetingness by no means destroys the sense of its ideal immortality. He sees that it is beyond and above the calculations of ordinary life—there is a wisdom of this world and a wisdom of love—for he has said—

[1] *The Adventures of Harry Richmond*, chap. lv.
[2] *Ask, is Love Divine.*

The young who avoid that region escape the title of Fool at the cost of a celestial crown.[1]

It is certainly in such expressions that some of the mystery of love is uttered, for it is not merely of this earth, earthy, but is divine, and a gleam of that world, ' where music and moonlight and feeling are one'. To Meredith it is inherently noble—the amplifier and purifier of passion. His expression—

> Passion is *noble strength on fire*.[2]

really represents this view, that love is human, but also more than human, because it echoes the music of wishes and hopes that are so far beyond adequate accomplishment. What it means is unknown—that it means something is certain. For perhaps they who love are nearer to the heart of life than we ; they dream dreams in daylight that enclose the world, we, in sluggish night, that enclose ourselves. There is a sentence of his, which goes far to explain this mixture of divinity and personality—

> Love may be celestial fire before it enters into the systems of mortals. It will then take the character of its place of abode, and we have to look not so much for the pure thing as for the passion.[3]

---

[1] *Diana of the Crossways*, chap. i.
[2] *Sandra Belloni*, chap. xliv.
[3] *The Tragic Comedians*, Introduction.

For we know the universal feelings of love, and we know also how completely personal and individual they are. There is no language that will explain it, for it transcends actuality in the mind of the lover.

And so, possibly, this is the reason that even impersonal interest in love does not really lie in the dissection of the passion nor in the wise and penetrating remarks arising therefrom, but rather in the thing itself and in the description of those emotions which we know very well are a climax of truth in a far deeper sense than remorseless and logical theories. The great figures of Meredith's creation are in love in no less a complete sense than they are in life, in fact it is then the same thing to them. The artist in Meredith has shown him how to treat love simply as a natural and necessary growth of life and not as one of those adjuncts or happenings which call for admirable moralizings. There is no more a special moral in the idea of being in love than there is in the idea of being alive.

I have meant all these remarks to mean this, that the true realization of love to the reader must be gained through the emotional and artistic side and not primarily through the moral side. For it is the romance element at the goal of life and therefore through romantic and inspired eyes must we follow it. Throughout his works Meredith has taken such views of love; he has entirely imagined it as the thing to be understood through the finer senses. His love scenes are not only beautifully filled with the spirit of the idea, but are outwardly surrounded by the actual reflection of the inner completeness. Nothing is wanting to make up that harmony to the reader, which must, in the very nature of love, appear to the lover. For it is in such wonderful thoughts of an immortal unity, that we come to their souls. For they hear a melody that subdues the world and enables them to see it through the rosy tints of an eternal benediction. Such a thing then has Meredith supposed love, and such briefly is his method of speaking of it. I believe there is no writer who has more entirely entered into its heart and spirit and given us descriptions with more enchanting and moving insight. For his sense of local and personal colouring is so strong that it has risen above the artificial atmosphere of the novel. Let me quote the first meeting of Lucy Desborough and Richard Feverel for a matchless and thrilling effect—

Above green flashing plunges of a weir, and shaken by the thunder below, lilies, golden and white, were swaying at anchor among the reeds. Meadow-sweet hung from the banks thick with weed and trailing bramble, and there also hung a daughter of earth. Her face was shaded by a broad straw hat with a flexible brim that left her lips and chin in the sun, and, sometimes nodding, sent forth a light of promising eyes. Across her shoulders, and behind, flowed large loose curls, brown in shadow, almost golden where the ray touched them. She was simply dressed, befitting decency and the season. On a closer inspection you might see that her lips were stained. This blooming young person was regaling on dewberries. They grew between the bank and the water. Apparently she found the fruit abundant, for her hand was making pretty progress to her mouth. Fastidious youth, which revolts at woman plumping her exquisite proportions on bread and butter, and would (we must suppose) joyfully have her scraggy to have her poetical, can hardly object to dewberries. Indeed the act of eating them is dainty and induces musing. The dewberry is a sister to the lotus, and an innocent sister. You eat: mouth, eye, and hand are occupied, and the undrugged mind free to roam. And so it was with the damsel who knelt there. The little skylark went up above her, all song, to the smooth southern cloud lying along the blue; from a dewy copse dark over her nodding hat the blackbird fluted, calling to her with thrice mellow note: the kingfisher flashed emerald out of green osiers: a bow-winged heron travelled aloft, seeking solitude; a boat slipped towards her, containing a dreamy youth, and still she plucked the fruit, and ate, and mused, as if no fairy prince were invading her territories, and as if she wished not for one, or knew not her wishes. Surrounded by the green shaven meadows, the pastoral summer buzz, the weir fall's thundering white, amid the breath and beauty of wild flowers, she was a bit of lovely human life in a fair setting; a terrible attraction. The magnetic youth leaned round to note his proximity to the weir-piles, and beheld the sweet vision. Stiller and stiller grew nature, as at the meeting of two electric clouds. Her posture was so graceful, that though he was making straight for the weir, he dared not dip a scull. Just then one enticing dewberry caught her eyes. He was floating by unheeded, and saw that her hand stretched low, and could not gather what it sought. A stroke from his right brought him beside her. The damsel glanced up dismayed, and her whole shape trembled over the brink. Richard sprang from his boat into the water. Pressing a hand beneath her foot, which she had thrust against the crumbling wet sides of the bank to save herself, he enabled her to recover her balance, and gain safe earth, whither he followed her.[1]

'Stiller and stiller grew nature as at the meeting of two electric clouds'—in such language dwells that something which defies time, the ever fresh, the ever aged. Follow then these lovers, in those sentences, than which there are none more glorious in our language, that tell of their plighting—

They have outflown philosophy. Their instinct has shot beyond the ken of science. They were made for their Eden.

'And this divine gift was in store for me!'

So runs the internal outcry of each, clasping each; it is their recurring refrain to the harmonies. How it illumined the years gone by and suffused the living Future!

'You for me: I for you!'

'We are born for each other!'

---

[1] *The Ordeal of Richard Feverel*, chap. xiv.

They believe that the angels have been busy about them from their cradles. The celestial hosts have worthily striven to bring them together. And, O victory! O wonder! after toil and pain, and difficulties exceeding, the celestial hosts have succeeded!

'Here we two sit who are written above as one!'

Pipe, happy Love! pipe on to these dear innocents!

The tide of colour has ebbed from the upper sky. In the West the sea of sunken fire draws back; and the stars leap forth, and tremble, and retire before the advancing moon, who slips the silver train of cloud from her shoulders, and, with her foot upon the pine-tops, surveys heaven.

'Lucy, did you never dream of meeting me?'

'O Richard! yes; for I remembered you.'

'Lucy! and did you pray that we might meet?'

'I did!'

Young as when she looked upon the lovers in Paradise, the fair Immortal journeys onward. Fronting her, it is not night but veiled day. Full half the sky is flushed. Not darkness, not day, but the nuptials of the two.

'My own! my own for ever! You are pledged to me? Whisper!'

He hears the delicious music.

'And you are mine?'

A soft beam travels to the fern covert under the pine-wood where they sit, and for answer he has her eyes: turned to him an instant, timidly fluttering over the depths of his, and then downcast; for through her eyes her soul is naked to him.

'Lucy! my bride! my life!'

The night-jar spins his dark monotony on the branch of the pine. The soft beam travels round them, and listens to their hearts. Their lips are locked.

Pipe no more, Love, for a time! Pipe as you will you cannot express their first kiss; nothing of its sweetness, and of the sacredness of it nothing. St. Cecilia up aloft, before the silver organ-pipes of Paradise, pressing fingers upon all the notes of which Love is but one, from her you may hear it.[1]

As they sat in that calm twilight, we know that some whisper of the ages was heard by them—a solemn and mysterious time. Around them the sky began to assume the symbol of their hearts' union, and the air the stillness of their hearts' peace. The earth seemed to be beating in unison with them and they were at one with nature. Such lovers have indeed ' outflown philosophy ', for they have entered upon an ethereal plane, which is not within the scheme of our comprehension. Read these few lines, where Lucy and Richard are upon the lake on a calm evening like this, and he, floating on the entrancing and nameless magnetism of the scene, for one moment is in the realm of the blest—

> The shadow of the cypress was lessening on the lake. The moon was climbing high. As Richard rowed the boat, Lucy sang to him softly. She sang first a fresh little French song, reminding him of a day when she had been asked to sing to him before, and he did not care to hear. ' Did I live ? ' he thinks. Then she sang to him a bit of one of those majestic old Gregorian chants, that, wherever you may hear them, seem to build up cathedral walls about you. The young man dropped the sculls. The strange solemn notes gave a religious tone to his love, and wafted him into the knightly ages and the reverential heart of chivalry.

---

[1] *The Ordeal of Richard Feverel*, chap. xix.

Hanging between two heavens on the lake; floating to her voice; the moon stepping over and through white shoals of soft high clouds above and below; floating to her voice—no other breath abroad! His soul went out of his body as he listened.[1]

It is beautiful and it is true.

That too is a glowing description in *The Shaving of Shagpat*, where Bhanavar and Almeryl lean from the balcony into the sultry Persian night and feel the passion and throbbing music of the darkness enter into them like another note to swell the chord of song—

Almeryl stretched his arm to the lattice, and drew it open, letting in the soft night wind, and the sound of the fountain, and the bulbul and the beam of the stars, and versed to her in the languor of deep love:

> Whether we die or we live,
>   Matters it now no more:
> Life has nought further to give:
>   Love is its crown and its core.
> Come to us either, we're rife—
>   Death or life!
>
> Death can take not away,
>   Darkness and light are the same:
> We are beyond the pale ray,
>   Wrapt in a rosier flame:
> Welcome which will to our breath—
>   Life or death!

So did these two lovers lute and sing in the stillness of the night, pouring into each other's ears melodies

---

[1] *The Ordeal of Richard Feverel*, chap. xx.

from the new sea of fancy and feeling that flowed through them. Ere they ceased their sweet interchange of tenderness, which was but one speech from one soul, a glow of light ran up the sky, and the edge of a cloud was fired; and in the blooming of dawn Almeryl hung over Bhanavar, and in his heart ached to see the freshness of her wondrous loveliness.[1]

Here again is that universal harmony which we know to be the background of emotions like these. The fragrant pulse and murmur of the night was but the counterpart of their own hearts. For love is strong to make itself the master of the occasion and throw its shadow not less outwardly than inwardly. It is far too personal to argue about, for it really means to each one of us something it has never meant to anyone else.

It seems to me that no other novelist, save Turgenieff, has treated love as Meredith has, for he, in his great descriptions, writes of it as from the internal and inspired standpoint. Far down in the heart of a man or a woman he notes the awakening of this passion, follows it, keeps fixed look upon all its intricate and strange turnings, understands its leavening influence, its intensity, tragic solemnity, and total power. To him a life thus swayed is seen in lights that have a direct and even

[1] *The Shaving of Shagpat*, 'The Story of Bhanavar.'

commanding communication with it. The workings of it are by no means voluntary and by no means necessarily conscious. And then at last when the moment of all existence is at hand, he is able to seize from the furnace of the mind the white hot and burning intensity of the passion ; then at last the romance and splendour of the lover's soul lie open before him.

I have elsewhere spoken of his extraordinary insight to character and of his poetical grasp of life and nature, and no doubt, such a junction must have helped to give him this unique perception of love and peculiar beauty of description. For it is the feeling that we have before us living people in surroundings vividly under the spell of their imagination, that so moves us in watching these scenes. In fact, it is the great atmosphere of love that makes it possible for outsiders to enter into something of its spirit. It is the intensest moment of the reality and omniscience of personality, the most dramatic and human of all the episodes of life, for in it the actual is triumphant and we know that all the shams and conventions of outlook sink away. Perhaps they are not lasting moments, but while they exist they are supremely and divinely real. For the most human in us is that which most nearly transcends humanity, and the most real, the most ethereal. Meredith has cleaved asunder the banter and the sentimentality that surround love-scenes, and we see before us the dawning and terrible emotions of which they are actually composed. Love is neither ridiculous nor feeble, it is simply the core and heart of life. As I have said in other words, it weaves into its fabric every outward and inward picture. That star mysteriously glittering through the solemn and darkening twilight becomes to him the messenger of love's divinity, that river rolling to the sea the whisper of love's endlessness. Not only is this so, but there is subtly thrown over everything an almost personal relationship with the soul of the lover. The following beautiful song is an apt illustration of this special frame of mind—

   Night like a dying mother,
     Eyes her young offspring, Day.
   The birds are dreamily piping,
     And O, my love, my darling!
   The night is life ebb'd away:
     Away beyond our reach!
   A sea that has cast us pale on the beach;
     Weeds with weeds and the pebbles
   That hear the lone tamarisk rooted in sand
                  Sway
   With the song of the sea to the land.[1]

---

[1] *By Morning Twilight.*

The boundless horizon of love is, at the very outset, tinged with the view that is not in ordinary life, perhaps indeed a view truer than the ones of ordinary life. There are many aspects under which it is possible to consider the idea of love and its effect upon character and circumstance, but the one aspect of universal and absorbing interest is just that one that is too fine and too elusive to describe. It is actually a greater thing to understand love than to understand about love, and a more marvellous thing to describe the action of it than the meaning of it. I am not sure whether in the whole of Meredith's works there is a single scene which more truly represents the real spirit of the abstract emotion, than this stanza from *Love in the Valley*—

All the girls are out with their baskets for the primrose ;
    Up lanes, woods through, they troop in joyful bands.
My sweet leads : she knows not why, but now she loiters,
    Eyes the bent anemones, and hangs her hands.
Such a look will tell that the violets are peeping,
    Coming the rose : and unaware a cry
Springs in her bosom for odours and for colour,
    Covert and the nightingale ; she knows not why.[1]

Suddenly and strangely there has dawned upon her a mystical flash, an echo of some-

---

[1] Stanza xi.

thing half caught in forgotten sunsets, and faintly heard in dark labyrinths of sleep. It is love that is stirring to make another existence leap past the transient present to an immortal goal. We know well that the joy of love is half pain. It is possibly because this goal is so retreating, and because there is lying a certain indefinable sadness in the deepest emotions. In the stanza I have just quoted this is noticeable, and we feel that there is a movement in the girl's thoughts dimly unhappy in the dim happiness of her mind. We see a side of this emotion also in the description of Nesta in *One of our Conquerors*—

> Nesta felt it, without asking whether she was loved. She was his. She had not a thought of the word of love or the being beloved. Showers of painful blissfulness went through her, as the tremours of a shocked frame, while she sat quietly, showing scarce a sign; and after he had let her hand go, she had the pressure on it. The quivering intense of the moment of his eyes and grasp was lord of her, lord of the day and of all days coming. That is how Love slays Death. Never did girl so give her soul.[1]

We cannot quite understand this sensation but we are aware that it is natural and true to reality. It is the thought of being on the brink of an unknown and rather terrible

[1] Chap. xxxviii.

uncertainty—the idea of standing over a dark and lonely gulf of unplumbed emotions. To look into eyes, intoxicating as wine, deep as night, shocks us and kindles us at the same instant. To feel that we are gliding from sensations that are of a present into those that are of an eternity, and from the darkness of our limitations into the starlight of immensity, is in us as an idea that is tragic. Now indeed is it true that beautiful melodies float upon the air and the sound of happy music is audible to us. The night cannot hold deeper mystery than do the souls of lovers nor diviner dreams than the hearts of those who love. For the lover draws to himself the stars and the spirit of all the earth and forms from them a fresh cosmos and a marvellous interpretation of the senses. None of those things which we comprehend as immortal are outside the grasp of his universal and harmonious brain, for now has he cast out upon a wider sea and knows that there is a something which is the elusive aim of all desire and pain and joy. Here truly it is with beauty and solemnity given by Meredith—

So, now the soft summer hours flew like white doves from off the mounting moon, and the lovers turned to go, all being still: even the noise of the waters still to their ears, as life that is muffled in sleep. They saw the cedar grey-edged under the moon ; and Night, that clung like a bat beneath its ancient open palms. The bordering sward about the falls shone silvery. In its shadow was a swan. These scenes are but beckoning hands to the hearts of lovers, waving them on to that Eden which they claim ; but when the hour has fled they know it ; and by the palpitating light in it they know that it holds the best of them.[1]

In this is the atmosphere that tells the tales of those stupendous moments, that time as of ' life that is muffled in sleep '.

I do not think a particular purpose would be served by making an analysis of different figures under this potent and almighty spell, as was done for instance in the case of tragedy. It would be a recital of practically every distinguishable character in these novels and poems, and to make them significant and realizable would require a very long and acute study into the influence of their respective personalities and environments. Nor, as I have already explained, is it my purpose to describe the different stages of the rise and fall of this passion and its action and re-action on personality. All this is of commanding interest but of a kind that is mainly psychological and intellectual, whereas surely the most tremendous conclusions are the poeti-

[1] *Sandra Belloni*, chap. xx.

ON LOVE

cal and, in a sense, emotional. For I have endeavoured to touch on love, as the universal and eternal force, and treat its personality from the impersonal standpoint. In other words I have treated it as one great whole and not as a million individual and passionate movements. To every one love is the same in that it is the expression of a sublimity, but to every one it is different in that it is the slave and the creation of intensely personal surroundings. The treatment of this second side of it, this side in which we see life and character and destiny, is to be found written about to some extent in different remarks scattered through this book; but I have not spoken of it here in a definite fashion, for I have had in view a different object. I have had in view the atmosphere of his comprehension of the ideal word love, not perhaps in the widest sense in which it includes every noble and forward step and every true and poetic thought, but in that thrilling world-wide sense, in which certain words, spoken perhaps faultily and with poor intonation, ring out yet a melody not unheard in paradise.

CHAPTER X

On Egoism, Sentimentalism and their Relationship

ALL students of Meredith know that he is the profoundest direct delineator of egoism in our, and probably any, language. That is to say, he has more deeply read the spirit of inherent selfishness and more accurately gauged its meanings and subtleties, than has any other writer. Not only in *The Egoist* itself, but in every one of his novels there is a sense at work to explore the egoism underlying and forming the structure of personality. To him it has become not merely the chance characteristic that one incongruous or peculiar figure might suggest but a definite and vital constituent in every life. He claims that it is one of the inborn legacies, and as such amenable to real philosophic research. He sees it as the great elemental instinct, educated by society to wear over this body of the primal such a polished coating of modernity, that many may have been led into the belief that it is one of the things society has formed instead of realizing what is the truth, that it was in existence ages before society was even imaginable. As he says with very remarkable acumen—

The Egoist is our fountain-head, primeval man : the primitive is born again, the elemental reconstituted. Born again, into new conditions, the primitive may be highly polished of men, and forfeit nothing save the roughness of his original nature. He is not only his own father, he is ours ; and he is also our son. We have produced him, he us. Such were we, to such are we returning ; not other, sings the poet, than one who toilfully works his shallop against the tide ' si brachia forte remisit : '—let him haply relax the labour of his arms, however high up the stream, and back he goes, ' in pejus,' to the early principle of our being, with seeds and plants, that are as carelessly weighed in the hand and as indiscriminately husbanded as our humanity.

Poets on the other side may be cited for an assurance that the primitive is not the degenerate ; rather is he a sign of the indestructibility of the race, of the ancient energy in removing obstacles to individual growth ; a sample of what we would be, had we his concentrated power. He is the original innocent, the pure simple. It is we who have fallen ; we have melted into Society, diluted our essence, dissolved. He stands in the midst monumentally, a landmark of the tough and honest old Ages, with the symbolic alphabet of striking arms and running legs, our early language, scrawled over his person, and the glorious first flint and arrow-head for his crest ; at once the spectre of the Kitchen-midden and our ripest issue.

But Society is about him. The occasional spectacle

of the primitive dangling on a rope has impressed his mind with the strength of his natural enemy ; from which uncongenial sight he has turned shuddering hardly less to behold the blast that is blown upon a reputation where one has been disrespectful of the many. By these means, through meditation on the contrast of circumstances in life, a pulse of imagination has begun to stir, and he has entered the upper sphere, or circle of spiritual Egoism ; he has become the civilized Egoist ; primitive still, as sure as man has teeth, but developed in his manner of using them.[1]

The civilized Egoist of whom he here speaks is, in other words, the sentimentalist. For sentimentalism to Meredith is the essence of present-day Egoism. I have said in my chapter on 'Insight into Character' that he has a far more kindly eye for the egoist than for the sentimentalist, and this is true. For the egoist is in some true sense a product of nature, existing as a demonstration of the survival of the fittest, and tinged to a considerable degree with the impersonality of Caliban or the Minotaur, but the sentimentalist is self-conscious and perfectly awake to what are his aims. The egoist is frequently unconscious of his egoism, the sentimentalist, in the bottom of his soul, is conscious of his sentimentalism. But indeed unconsciousness is in such a case not

[1] *The Egoist*, chap. xxxix.

much more than a semi-excuse. Too long has the reign of egoism flourished, to suppose that education must not have noticed the results. Though Meredith can see its better side as a common phenomenon and can treat it therefore as an abstract question in the philosophy of manners, he is not blind to its heavy and fateful influence on history and individuality. As he remarks—

... The stench of the trail of Ego in our History.[1]
which is not altogether an optimistic sentence. Indeed Egoism, even in its crudest and most primitive form, is not an inspiring study. It is simply the struggle to gain for yourself what others have an equal right to, in fact, the effort to live for yourself alone. All people have born in them a secret feeling of their own importance and a terrible desire to get their way through every obstacle.

Egoism dwells in the contemplation of itself, and is, in the very structure of its being, blind to its own limitations. Meredith writes in the introductory chapter to *The Egoist*, 'through very love of self himself he slew'— a line which is packed with irony. Nothing is too out of the way to be used for its support

[1] *Beauchamp's Career*, chap. xxix, written by Dr Shrapnel.

or progress. That is why it so soon refines itself under the hands of society. It is only too anxious to make use of any help for its own purposes, and only too willing to pour itself into any mould that will further its own projects. For it is that cunning appetite of life that can hide itself under a thousand disguises and involve itself in a hundred sophisms, without ever really losing sight of the cold and steely reason of its manoeuvrings. The more civilized it becomes the more personal it also becomes. This is, of course, a natural result, and is the old tale of awakening intelligence.

Why then does Meredith call a refined egoist, a sentimentalist? For this reason. Such egoism embraces not only a man's mind, but his conscience. It is like the air, evenly pressing on every available space. Now the more educated the egoist becomes, the more he grasps the significance of egoism, but the more he also grasps the excellent state of the egoist to himself. The result of this is that he is in a perpetual condition of trying to deceive himself and make himself comfortable. He appeases his conscience with sops and is for ever endeavouring to cast a film over his eyes and suppose to himself that all is perfectly well. He is a sentimentalist because he has a sickly hope that everything is right, without making unpleasant digs beneath the surface (whether of his own mind or the outside world), and he is an egoist because his hope is mainly there in order to soothe and lull his intelligence. For, as a rule, he is a long way from being a fool and knows what the problems are, and assumes a pretence that things will come right, and that there is a time for reform and the new and final repentance. His life passes in an understood resolve with himself to start afresh at some future date—the present being simply the preparation and unavoidable prelude. But he can never quite persuade himself that he is in earnest—as I have already said, somewhere in the depth of his mind he knows that he is not. To quote Meredith again—

> Sentimentalists are they who seek to enjoy without incurring the Immense Debtorship for a thing done.[1]

This really is his attitude: he is attempting to reverse that fundamental law of value for something received.

Meredith sees the sentimentalist as a man

[1] *The Ordeal of Richard Feverel*, chap. xxiv.

222 ON EGOISM, SENTIMENTALISM

false to nature. He is for ever trying to fit her into his scheme of weak and mundane emotions. The sentimentalist is wrapt up in himself, and not only does not understand the impersonality of nature but by some strange hallucination imagines that she has him, or should have him, in especial regard. Though highly strung to weep over himself, and nervously alive to heroic poses and to a true comprehension and a true joy in what is great and noble (for it is quite a mistake to suppose that he is pure mountebank or deceiver) he is yet cruel in procuring for himself that eminence from which he may indulge these wishes and thoughts. He is in fact utterly unscrupulous, but always glosses over his unscrupulousness by an excuse and really tries to pretend to himself that the end is worthy of the means, or that it is the last time. He not only has to explain his actions to the world, he has to explain them to himself, and his internal arguments are ghosts that haunt him for ever.

Nor need we suppose that this spirit of sentimentalism would not foster great virtues of the immediate and positive type, were the audience of a fit description. The sentimentalist wants to live in the admiring glances of the present. For instance, a thing like courage, that at once attracts attention, would eminently come under this rule. Look at Wilfrid Pole.[1] I doubt whether in all Meredith's books there is a more complete example of the sentimental egoist; and yet he is an extremely brave man, and fitted apparently with many attractive qualities; or in his love affairs is it a case of this ?—

. . . women who are called coquettes make their conquests not of the best of men; but men who are Egoists have *good* women for their victims; women on whose devoted constancy they feed; they drink it like blood.[2]

For there is a kind of base self-consciousness about the sentimentalist that saves him from the ordinary blunders and snares that, once committed, awaken repulsion. He understands the art of appearing other than he is, or at any rate of presenting only the one side of a nature that is complex in its very contrasts.

Remember that in his desire to shine before himself as well as outwardly, he shows a sincerity, the real meaning of which it is hard to perceive, for even to himself it is hidden in a hundred folds.

[1] *Sandra Belloni* and *Vittoria*.
[2] *The Egoist*, chap. xvi, spoken by Clara Middleton.

The sentimentalist, as Meredith says of Wilfrid Pole, can bind himself to eternity, but he cannot bind himself to to-morrow morning. Living fiercely and eternally in the present, his life is a make-believe that he is living properly in the to-come. He likes to see around him peace and prosperity, because they all react upon the inward state of his comfort. He would imagine a harmony of the World, in which he was the prime mover, standing calmly by with a beneficial smile as all things revolved round about him. It is a very delightful idea, and one method of saying, ' I should be honest if I had £5,000 a year '. Meredith has the custom of showing us the sentimentalist in that stage (awkward for him) when he is trying to reach these happy heights, and when his smile is not altogether so sweet or his actions altogether so blameless. In fact he shows us the sentimentalist in the struggle of existence. Had I not already made an examination of a representative egoist in my chapter on ' Insight into Character ', I should have been inclined to give here a description of some typical figures of egoism and sentimentalism from the works of George Meredith. Many characters suggest themselves—Sir Austin Feverel,[1] Sir Purcell Barrett,[2] the ladies Pole,[3] Wilfrid Pole,[4] Edward Blancove,[5] Sir Willoughby Patterne,[6] Sir Lukin Dunstane,[7] Victor Radnor,[8] Lord Fleetwood.[9] They are not of course all built according to the same pattern, and the grades between egoism and sentimentalism may be wide, but they would all have to be included in any searching report into the subject as a whole. For instance, Professor Edgar in an able paper in the *National Review* for September, 1907, goes to the length of seeing four distinct types of sentimentalist in the novel of *Sandra Belloni*—' the worldly sentimentality of the Pole sisters, the patriotic sentimentality, and hence more excusable, of Merthyr Powys and his sister, the tragic sentimentality of disillusionment in Purcell Barrett, and the amorous sentimentality of Wilfrid Pole!' All this is very suggestive and goes to show the danger of assuming a label to represent an individuality. Naturally egoism and sentimentalism are enormously altered and varied

---

[1] *The Ordeal of Richard Feverel.* [2] *Sandra Belloni.*
[3] *Sandra Belloni.* [4] *Sandra Belloni* and *Vittoria.*
[5] *Rhoda Fleming.*
[6] *The Egoist.* [7] *Diana of the Crossways.*
[8] *One of our Conquerors.* [9] *The Amazing Marriage.*

by the personalities in which they work. They will seize upon the weakest spot. Again some ground is most fruitful for cultivation, other ground has a natural antipathy, either open or in abeyance.

Meredith has attempted to lay bare not alone the actions but the motives of the egoist. In the minute and powerful study of Sir Willoughby Patterne for example, he has had his brain before him like the sections of a puzzle and has gradually and brilliantly evolved the picture of an egoist. He is the psychologist of society and nature—intent upon observing the laws that govern both and of noticing where they part company. Not only has he to say that the sentimentalist exists, but he has to say why he exists; not only has he to destroy, but he has to build up. The unmasking of a meanness is a negative way of pointing to the remedy, and the description of its converse is a positive way. They are two weapons constantly in Meredith's hands.

The sentimental egoist is a man not merely, as I have remarked, false to nature in Meredith's view, but false to himself. In his half-sincere efforts to reveal to himself his own mind, he is always aware that he is only half-sincere, or at any rate, some proportion of sincere that falls short of the real thing. For every layer he removes he recedes one layer deeper into sophistry. The tragic moment at length arrives when he is unable to pierce the veil of himself. It is a kind of stagnant triumph to his life's aim, but it is a bitter one, because he knows that he has lost the kingdom of himself. It may be possible to imagine a man too blinded to think about these matters, but even so, he must almost certainly begin to see in his actions nothing but a perpetual repetition of the ceaseless ego. It is a barren end. The worst of it is, that though the disillusionment of such people may be accomplished at times, there is little chance of any cure. It is too inherent, behind all its individual idiosyncrasy. Both Sir Willoughby Patterne [1] and Wilfrid Pole [2] (the two best instances in all these books) are shown to themselves in the light of others, but where is the permanent change ? Sir Willoughby's one effort is to keep himself where he stood in the eyes of the county, Wilfrid Pole's to win at any price his own happiness. The main result of their unmasking is to make them weep over them-

[1] *The Egoist.*   [2] *Sandra Belloni* and *Vittoria.*

selves and feverishly coin new positions in which they shall at last appear as the smiling and benevolent victors.

To Meredith sentimentalism is a form of mock sentiment, developed largely to excuse a view of life which we know to be morally untenable. His own sentence—

> All these false sensations, peculiar to men, concerning the soiled purity of woman, the lost innocence, the brand of shame upon her, which are commonly the foul sentimentalism of such as can be too eager in the chase of corruption when occasion suits, and are another side of pruriency, not absolutely foreign to the best of us in youth . .[1]

is an almost fierce commentary upon this side of the question. This hideous mask of feeling has to be trampled for ever into the dust. There is no good talking about advance whilst such thoughts can find a restful harbour in our brains. As long as falseness dominates, because we determine not to look the issue in the face, there is a cessation to progress—we are anchored to ourselves. It is not therefore surprising that Meredith has fought with such earnest and keen words to awaken us to our natural tendency towards sentimental egoism, and has shown us in his startling and deep analysis the trend of the egoistic outlook.

[1] *Rhoda Fleming*, chap. xxx.

CHAPTER XI

The Comic Spirit

THE spirit of comedy runs through the whole of Meredith's work. On it he has based a philosophy of the race as original in the abstract as it is penetrating in the reality. In the brilliant *Essay on Comedy* he has laid down with great nicety the laws that govern it, and I cannot do better than quote a few sentences—

> A society of cultivated men and women is required wherein ideas are current and the perceptions quick, that he may be supplied with matter and an audience. The semi-barbarism of merely giddy communities, and feverish emotional periods, repel him ; and also a state of marked social inequality of the sexes ; nor can he whose business is to address the mind be understood where there is not a moderate degree of intellectual activity.

This gives us the first requisite of the comic stage. Comedy is, in fact, only possible where the minds of all the actors are in a state of equal and rather distinct cultivation. The drawing-room is the home of the comic spirit. Meredith has himself said as much. It is perhaps the assurance of this that has caused him to make such frequent mention of the aristocratic upper classes. For such give in perfection the special social atmosphere (not necessarily intellectual, but well-bred, serenely mannered, and above all, wide-awake to the nuances) in which comedy flourishes. In the same way, the gift of understanding what is comic is a cultivated gift. You can only possess it in excelsis through comprehension of the aims and feelings of polite society. I do not mean by this that the field of comedy is narrow in the abstract, but only in the particular. In the abstract it embraces the whole world, in the particular it definitely clings to the type in which it finds distinctest representation.

It is easy enough to confound with comedy, such things as irony, satire, humour, and until these have been defined, the meaning of the word may remain cloudy. Here is Meredith's own comparison—

> If you detect the ridicule, and your kindliness is chilled by it, you are slipping into the grasp of satire.
> If instead of falling foul of the ridiculous person with a satiric rod, to make him writhe and shriek aloud, you prefer to sting him under a semi-caress, by which he

THE COMIC SPIRIT

shall in his anguish be rendered dubious whether indeed anything has hurt him, you are an engine of Irony.

If you laugh all round him, tumble him, roll him about, deal him a smack, and drop a tear on him, own his likeness to you and yours to your neighbour, spare him as little as you shun, pity him as much as you expose, it is a spirit of Humour that is moving you.

The Comic, which is the perceptive, is the governing spirit, awakening and giving aim to those powers of laughter but it is not to be confounded with them : it enfolds a thinner form of them, differing from satire : in not sharply driving into the quivering sensibilities, and from humour, in not comforting them and tucking them up, or indicating a broader than the range of this bustling world to them.[1]

It clearly gives the scope of each word. Comedy is the view that the still and penetrative watcher obtains from the observation of the machine of this planet. There is nothing more detached than the sense of comedy. Meredith skilfully voices the thoughts of all who understand it—

> The laughter of Comedy is impersonal and of unrivalled politeness, nearer a smile ; often no more than a smile, It laughs through the mind, for the mind directs it ; and it might be called the humour of the mind.[2]

It is the smile that dies into a thought.

Few things cause greater misunderstanding than the loose usage so frequently made of expressions like humour, wit, and comedy. They are, in truth, words that have highly

[1] *Essay on Comedy.*   [2] *Essay on Comedy.*

individual and exact meanings, and though in actual experience there are many events which are comprised of compounds of them, still in theory they each of them stand alone as representative of an exact phase and condition of thought. Nothing could be more foolish than to suppose comedy to mean something that was necessarily in itself amusing. It is infinitely wider and more philosophical. Meredith says—

> To laugh at everything is to have no appreciation of the Comic of Comedy.[1]

Tragedy might be comic, hilarity probably would not be. Comedy is the science of discovering the heart of society, as represented by the individuals that form it, and, in a wider sense, of looking at the universe in general from the point of aloofness that can follow all its windings without being in itself subject to its influences. And, as I have said elsewhere, the comic spirit is one of the weapons of sanity. It keeps before our eyes the sense of proportion, and shows us the path of common sense. Let me quote Meredith again—

> For Folly is the natural prey of the Comic, known to

---

[1] *Essay on Comedy.*

it in all her transformations, in every disguise; and it is with the springing delight of hawk over heron, hound after fox, that it gives her chase, never fretting, never tiring, sure of having her, allowing her no rest.[1]

Comedy is the untiring foe of falseness along the track of progress. It sprang into being from civilization and it is the servant of civilization. Meredith has so convincingly explained his own perception of comedy and the fine and subtle points of the comic spirit that it is quite unnecessary for me to try any longer to clear the path of understanding. As a matter of fact, I am quite prepared to hear that chaos and not clarity has been achieved. The difference between comedy in the abstract and comedy in the concrete may well enough appear the difference between two things quite unrelated. The explanation may be put like this. In the abstract you can assume that you alone are aware of the sentient philosophy underlying life, and consequently can keep, on the strength of that, a kind of calm look on the struggles and fever of existence; while, in the concrete, you can see through the same underlying spirit that the leisured and cultivated alone possesses in its full purity, the elu-

[1] *Essay on Comedy.*

sive nicety of aim, the intense susceptibility to hints, which is the fit pasturage of the comic spirit.

It is important that every student of Meredith's philosophy of life should carefully study the *Essay on Comedy* before attempting even a partial definition of the meaning and scope of his teaching. For comedy is twined into the broad basis of his view of his fellows. It is difficult to grasp how far such a spirit is a negative, as well as a positive force; how far, that is to say, it influences the other formatives of a philosophic outlook on life and nature, as well as being in itself one of the most considerable of them. It is such an idea that leads us to see the essential falseness of any abstract word used in relation to anything human, in its individual sense and no other wise. When we say that a thing is tragic or comic, we are in reality using these words in a very different sense to their dictionary terminology. Nothing in this world could stand in itself as an actual representative of any word so arbitrary. An event may, probably will, show an essential and culminating feature, and by that we name it, but of course there are a hundred subsidiary influences that have gone to form the impression. And in such a way the comic spirit is one of the presiding elements of the outlook of George Meredith; sometimes clearly, unmistakably apparent, sometimes merely impersonally, negatively so.

Molière and Meredith are probably the two supreme comic writers in literature. They, of all others, have the profoundest insight to the elemental passions in that cultured and perfumed form which may be said to represent the mind of society. For the comic spirit is a kind of intellectual iron-hand-in-the-velvet-glove, and is as keen-visioned as it is polished.

When we have studied the tenets of the *Essay on Comedy*, we can then start a philosophical analysis of the development of these ideas throughout the series of social comedies which constitute so large a share of his work. It is quite noticeable that with the advent of *The Egoist*, the bounds of comedy become more defined. The comedies of the earlier periods are more rollicking, if I may use such an expression. Much of *Evan Harrington* for instance is almost farcical comedy; *Harry Richmond* is romantic comedy, and so on. But with *The Egoist*, the type of true mental comedy becomes paramount. The elimination of unnecessary detail is logically insisted on. Meredith says—

> Comedy is a game played to throw reflections upon social life, and it deals with human nature in the drawing-room of civilized men and women, where we have no dust of the struggling outer world, no mire, no violent crashes, to make the correctness of the representation convincing. Credulity is not wooed through the impressionable senses; nor have we recourse to the small circular glow of the watchmaker's eye to raise in bright relief minutest grains of evidence for the routing of incredulity. The Comic Spirit conceives a definite situation for a number of characters, and rejects all accessories in the exclusive pursuit of them and their speech.[1]

The aim is to concentrate on those figures surrounded by the comic spirit the full light of publicity, and really follow out the result of actions. Nothing is to distract the attention, nothing hinder the judgment. The comic spirit is pitiless where it finds its prey. It discards all trappings that might lead us from the heart of its victim, and seeks simply to unmask the soul, and bring about the fulfilment of its sentences. The differences between the comedy of the earlier period and of the later might be well represented by two quotations. Here is a sentence from *Evan Harrington*—

---

[1] *The Egoist*, Prelude.

Thinking he was apprehended, Mr Goren said : ' I'm going down to-night to take care of the shop. He's to be buried in his old uniform. You had better come with me by the night-coach, if you would see the last of him, young man.'

Breaking an odd pause that had fallen, the Countess cried aloud, suddenly :

' In his uniform ! '

Mr Goren felt his arm seized and his legs hurrying him some paces into isolation. ' Thanks ! thanks ! ' was murmured in his ear. ' Not a word more. Evan cannot bear it. Oh ! you are good to have come, and we are grateful. My father ! my father ! '

She had to tighten her hand and wrist against her bosom to keep herself up. She had to reckon in a glance how much Rose had heard, or divined. She had to mark whether the Count had understood a syllable. She had to whisper to Evan to hasten away with the horrible man. She had to enliven his stunned senses, and calm her own.[1]

It is just a little too boisterous to have pleased the Meredith of a later age. What really is comic is the remark, ' In his uniform ! ' and the flood of colour it throws over the mind of the Countess. And here is a quotation from *The Egoist*—

' You are cold, my love ? you shivered.'

' I am not cold,' said Clara. ' Some one, I suppose, was walking over my grave.'

The gulf of a caress hove in view like an enormous billow hollowing under the curled ridge. She stooped to a buttercup ; the monster swept by. ' Your grave ! ' he exclaimed over her head ; ' my own girl ! '[2]

---

[1] Chap. iv.   [2] Chap. xiii.

It is very quiet, but it is very penetrating.

As would naturally be supposed from what I said above, the comic spirit makes a constant appearance in every one of Meredith's books, whether the main inspiration be comic or tragic. Over all of them lies the sense of comedy in the abstract, and over all of them, in certain individual episodes at any rate, the sense of comedy in the concrete. It is in fact as much a part of his mental equipment as is the sense of poetry. He frequently dilates upon the value of the comic poet and sees therein that sanely lyrical view of things which seems to him the aim of the generations.

It is not my intention to make any detailed examination of the comedy of George Meredith. I want rather to point to the path that such an examination should follow. But I think an end would be served by mentioning a few of the more comic situations in which his works abound. *Evan Harrington*, for instance, of which we have just been speaking, brims over with comedy of a joyous and fresh description. The various scenes at Beckley, when the Harringtons are in the heart of the hostile camp, are rich in effects. Here is Meredith's typical social battlefield—the haunt of the comic spirit. The triumphs

THE COMIC SPIRIT 239

and awful moments of the Countess de Saldar are essays in the emotions of the comic. It is what you might call a joyous book, full of hearty but thoughtful laughter. In *Harry Richmond* and *Beauchamp's Career* the spirit of comedy, though keenly wakeful, is more subservient to the needs of a wide plot. The setting of *Harry Richmond* is too romantic to be the ideal background of comedy, the setting of *Beauchamp's Career* too obviously serious. Nevertheless the social warfare is in both of them conspicuously alert. But it is in *Sandra Belloni* we come upon the ripe fruit of the comedy of the first stage. Lady Gosstre is superb. The garden party at Besworth,[1] where the three Miss Poles are so conscious of what must be done and so anxiously watchful of the great lady's every gesture, is unalloyed and delicious comedy. In this special line it is probably his crowning achievement. In fact the setting of the book is an example of what is real food for the comic spirit. The idea of the ladies Pole, with their fine shades of understanding, scheming night and day for the smiles of the county, is that of a brilliant imagination for the comic. The social atmosphere of

[1] Chap. xxxi.

this novel involves a true understanding of what are the essentials of comedy. It is indeed when the position for the presentation of any noticeable feature is particularly good that we can perhaps best observe the power of the artist. For then any false move tends to have a touch of crudeness that might not be so marked in conditions less perfect. It is such a book that shows Meredith's fine and judicious handling of comedy. The three short stories written in the late 70's, *The House on the Beach*, *The Case of General Ople and Lady Camper*, *The Tale of Chloe*, are further instances of consummate comedy. Though peculiarly interesting as being direct forerunners in date of *The Egoist*, they have no special affinity either with it or the earlier novels. They are altogether lighter than anything else he has written, though in *The Tale of Chloe* there is a touch of such poignant, even if insubstantial, tragedy, that the comic spirit is finally swallowed by the tragic. With *The Egoist*, Meredith's comedy becomes more mental and less obvious. The spirit of comedy is shown more deeply laid in the basis of character, instead of being to some degree the result of whims. Sir Willoughby Patterne is the prey of the comic muse, and not merely its servant. In the former books, we feel that the *dramatis personae* partially realize their positions, here we feel that they are the centre of an unconscious drama. Of course this is not true in its full significance, but there is a feeling that the comic tends here to become more philosophic, and less personal, and that the actors are not so much capable of commanding their destinies as they were in the other books. Perhaps it would be more accurate to say that with *The Egoist* comedy took to itself another office, for after all, much of the same spirit that is in *Sandra Belloni* is in this novel and the ones that followed. The conversations of Mrs Mount Stuart Jenkinson,[1] for instance, are of the same brood as those of Lady Gosstre,[2] and we have seen Ladies Busshe and Culmer [3] before. The plot of *The Egoist* is concentrated to a very high degree and an accurate light plays upon all the figures and searches out every weak spot and inherent blemish. The comic spirit, never benevolent in this aspect, is here simply an instrument of truth at all costs, and consequently little apt to be hoodwinked by sentimentalism or egoism.

[1] *The Egoist.*   [2] *Sandra Belloni.*   [3] *The Egoist.*

It encircles the lives of the characters in a way so circumstantial and exact that it marks a new departure in the treatment of the comic. Following *The Egoist* we get *The Tragic Comedians,* an attempt not altogether successful but significant and arresting along similar lines of comic comprehension. *Diana of the Crossways* has scenes of glittering comedy, but here again the plot does not fully lay itself out to comic treatment on a concise plan. Much the same may be said of the three latest novels of all, *One of our Conquerors, Lord Ormont and His Aminta,* and *The Amazing Marriage.*

Such then is a very brief outline of some of the more outstanding features and scenes of comedy in some of Meredith's novels. Its very briefness makes it inexact, not only from the great amount of matter untouched, but from the evident weakness of such short descriptions. Still, it may help people a little to know what to look for, and where to look for it, in tracing the comic spirit throughout George Meredith's works.

CHAPTER XII

Sense of Humour

THE difference between humour and comedy is broadly speaking this, that humour is democratic and obvious and comedy is mental and full of aloofness. Comedy is abstract, humour is concrete. For although real humour is subtle, still it is a subtlety dwelling on the surface and open to the sky. In the beginning of the last chapter I gave Meredith's own comparison of these two words, and no better step could be taken than a reference back to that extract. Humour makes us laugh and is in the best sense a jolly emotion. The capability and comprehension of it are inherent in every class and it is really the democratic sense of good feeling. You cannot instil humour into anyone who has not got it, but you find it, in greater or less degree, in every position. Primarily it is the sanity of the soil—and of all qualities it is that which most appears to spring fully armed from the soil. Meredith has that true sense of humour that leaves no sting. With him, it is frequently embodied in wit, which although not popular or democratic, is a usual mouthpiece for the higher grades of it. Of course wit need by no means be coupled with humour. The novels of Thomas Love Peacock are extremely witty but it is doubtful whether they could be called humorous, and the sayings of such raconteurs as Sir William Harcourt in real life or Simeon Fenellan [1] in fiction are certainly the first, without being necessarily the second. But still the witty saying has frequently an extremely humorous significance. Here for instance is a remark that is both witty and humorous—

To think of herself as personally disliked by a nobleman stupefied Mrs. Pagnell . . [2]

and here is another—

He was of a morality to reprobate the erring dame while he enjoyed the incidents.[3]

There have been many great humorists in the world since the days of Rabelais, and a singularly universal idea of what humour really is has been evolved. But in such a

---

[1] *One of our Conquerors.*
[2] *Lord Ormont and His Aminta*, chap. vi.
[3] *The Egoist*, chap. xxv.

word there is a general idea of what we all mean, and a very particular presentation of that idea by everyone who uses it. Lewis Carroll and George Meredith might each describe a fat man solemnly running to catch a train in a way quite obviously humorous and yet quite obviously entirely different. Let us suppose that two men had a sense of humour exactly the same and one were to read Lewis Carroll's description of the fat man, and one were to read George Meredith's description. These men would both say they had been reading real humour. And thus, although they have the same standards of humour, they see it in two things that are very unlike. This is one of these rather strange examples that shows the great breadth of a sense like this, only provided that it does ring true. For it would be quite possible to write about the fat man without making us do anything but yawn, and so the argument that it is simply the idea of a fat man running that is humorous does not apply with any particular force. Neither of these men would for one moment be misled by any pretence at humour, but where it actually exists there indeed is great latitude of perception.

The man without a sense of humour is a man lacking imagination. Fanatics, bigots, dogmatists and fools—these are the ranks from which they are recruited. It is one of the most difficult things to argue about, because it actually is there or is not—and you cannot make the blind see if the nerve is gone.

Much of the wider meaning of humour is seen in the avoidance of bad taste in other directions, for it has negative qualities of a high order. Sentimentalism and vulgarity cannot live in the light of humour and would be impossible were it understood by everybody. Humour in this view is really the admission that we are no more lords of the earth than anyone else, that we are one and all of us part of the same humanity. It is indeed the sense of proportion and comparative fitness. Like comedy it has an abstract and a personal side, and the understanding of one is largely the understanding of the other. In the abstract it is the great asset of law and order, and in the concrete it is the great asset of seeing the absurdity of many things without losing sight of their underlying strong humanity. Everywhere it is the soured and supercilious mind that is incapable of seeing the humorous, or at least of seeing it with a spirit of humour in itself equal to the spirit of humour in the thing under review.

Meredith is not a professedly humorous writer. The cast of his mind is too epigrammatic for the full development of the talent, but that he has the vital understanding of what it is, is apparent. We can observe it especially in the words he puts into the mouths of countrymen and the great joy he takes in their sayings. He has seen how native to the soil humour is and how inborn in those who live on the soil. It is not merely the feeling of delight we cannot help having at their naïve remarks and actions, but an admission that they are in themselves deeply humorous. They have, as it were, an elemental spirit of humour with roots far in the very system of their nature. Master Gammon, that memorable ' veteran of the fields ', is a very good example of my meaning. A spirit of grim humour surrounds him like a coat of armour, and it is impossible to say whether he is not having the laugh of you (but what an emotionless, inward laugh) when you think you are having the laugh of him. Do you not remember his conflict with Mrs. Sumfit about the tea ?—

Her hope was reduced to the prolonging of the service of tea, with Master Gammon's kind assistance.

'Four, marm,' said her inveterate antagonist, as he finished that amount, and consequently put the spoon in his cup.

Mrs Sumfit rolled in her chair.

'O Lord, Mas' Gammon! Five, I say; and never a cup less so long as here you've been.'

'Four, marm. I don't know,' said Master Gammon, with a slow nod of his head, 'that ever I took five cups of tea at a stretch. Not runnin'.'

'I *do* know, Mas' Gammon. And ought to; for don't I pour out to ye? It's five you take, and please, your cup if'll you'll hand it over.'

'Four's my number, marm,' Master Gammon reiterated resolutely. He sat like a rock.

'If they was dumplin's,' moaned Mrs Sumfit, 'not four, no, nor five, 'd do till enough you'd had, and here we might stick to our chairs, but you'd go on and on; you know you would.'

'That's eatin', marm;' Master Gammon condescended to explain the nature of his habits. 'I'm reg'lar in my drinkin'.'

Mrs Sumfit smote her hands together. 'O Lord, Mas' Gammon, the wearisomest old man I ever come across is you. More tea's in the pot, and it ain't watery, and you won't be comfortable. May you get forgiveness from above! is all I say, and I say no more. Mr Robert, perhaps you'll be so good as let me help you, sir? It's good tea, and my Dody,' she added, cajolingly, 'my home girl'll tell us what she saw. I'm pinched and starved to hear.' [1]

He is a slow, caustic, inscrutable old man. Andrew Hedger on the other hand is as amusing but has not the same depth. He is even rather

[1] *Rhoda Fleming*, chap. xiii.

SENSE OF HUMOUR

a wind-bag and can talk with great eloquence about food. But his philosophy of things is profoundly natural, and never more so than when he makes that noteworthy assertion, 'Ah could eat hog a solid hower'. Here is the full passage—

> They were all, and Andrew Hedger among them, the most entranced and profoundly reverent, observing the dissection of a pig.
> Unable to awaken his hearing, Redworth jogged his arm, and the shake was ineffective until it grew in force.
> 'I've no time to lose; have they told you the way?'
> Andrew Hedger yielded his arm. He slowly withdrew his intent fond gaze from the fair outstretched white carcase, and with drooping eyelids, he said: 'Ah could eat hog a solid hower!'
> He had forgotten to ask the way, intoxicated by the aspect of the pig; and when he did ask it, he was hard of understanding, given wholly to his last glimpses.[1]

I can imagine some people calling Andrew Hedger a materialist of the grossest description, but that would be almost a calumny. His materialism verges on idealism. I do not say that the subject of hogs is one capable of very ideal treatment, but certainly it is one capable of very unideal treatment, so that the merit should be in proportion to the opportunity. Andrew Hedger grows lyrical on the subject of

---

[1] *Diana of the Crossways*, chap. viii.

pigs, or as one should perhaps admit with some sadness, on the subject of eating pigs—

'Hog's my feed,' said Andrew Hedger. The gastric springs of eloquence moved him to discourse, and he unburdened himself between succulent pauses. 'They've killed him early. He's fat; and he might ha' been fatter. But he's fat. They've got their Christmas ready, that they have. Lord! you should see the chitterlings, and the sausages hung up to and along the beams. That's a crown for any dwellin'! They runs 'em round the top of the room—it's like a May-day wreath in old times. Home-fed hog! They've a treat in store, they have. And snap your fingers at the world for many a long day. And the hams! They cure their own hams at that house. Old style! That's what I say of a hog. He's good from end to end, and beats a Christian hollow. Everybody knows it and owns it?'[1]

He is really an admirable man, though inclined to be a little too discursive at inconvenient moments. We may recall to mind also the conversation between the tinker and speed-the-plough, in *Richard Feverel*—

From the weather theme they fell upon the blessings of tobacco; how it was the poor man's friend, his company, his consolation, his comfort, his refuge at night, his first thought in the morning.
'Better than a wife!' chuckled the tinker. 'No curtain-lecturin' with a pipe. Your pipe an't a shrew.'
'That be it!' the other chimed in. 'Your pipe doan't mak' ye out wi' all the cash Saturday evenin.'

---

[1] *Diana of the Crossways*, chap. viii.

SENSE OF HUMOUR

'Take one,' said the tinker, in the enthusiasm of the moment, handing a grimy short clay. Speed-the-plough filled from the tinker's pouch, and continued his praises.

'Penny a day, and there y'are, primed! Better than a wife? Ha, ha!'

'And you can get rid of it, if ye wants to, and when ye wants,' added tinker.

'So ye can!' Speed-the-Plough took him up. 'And ye doan't want for to. Leastways, t'other case. I means pipe.'

'And,' continued tinker, comprehending him perfectly, 'it don't bring repentance after it.'

'Not nohow, master, it doan't! And '—Speed-the-Plough cocked his eye—'it doan't eat up half the victuals, your pipe doan't.'[1]

It has that racy, natural humour which especially appeals to Meredith. The way Speed-the-plough mixes up his meaning but is perfectly understood by the tinker, and knows that he will be perfectly understood, is a masterly touch on the springs of laughter. John Thresher in *Harry Richmond*,[2] and the tramp in *The Egoist*,[3] must also be added to this gallery of notables.

Of course it is extremely easy to smile in a superior way at these people, but by doing this and this alone you miss their true significance. They are in the bywaters of mental progress but they are not in the bywaters of nature. They are probably nearer to nature

[1] Chap. iii.   [2] Chap. iii.   [3] Chap. xxvi.

than we are and contain certain natural characteristics that it would be as well for us if we were to study. Humour so emanates from them because they are not full of complicated thoughts and uneasy aspirations. They have that genuine gift, the philosophy of content, and a kind of inherent comprehension of the smallness of knowledge.

No one is more keenly analytical of the absurd than Meredith. His wide perception of phases of our modern social life has awakened in him an acute sense of the ridiculous. For instance, take this quotation—

> Two other sacrifices were offered at the piano after Laura Tinley. Poor victims of ambition, they arranged their dresses, smiled at the leaves, and deliberately gave utterance to the dreadful nonsense of the laureates of our drawing-rooms.[1]

You cannot help laughing, not only at the picture, but at the perfect truth of the picture. And here again in the following one, you might well say he has grasped the spirit of the suburban mind—

> The place he fell upon is only to be described in the tongue of auctioneers, and for the first week after taking it he modestly followed them by terming it bijou. In time, when his own imagination, instigated by a state of something more than mere contentment, had been at

---

[1] *Sandra Belloni*, chap. iv.

SENSE OF HUMOUR

work on it, he chose the happy phrase, ' a gentlemanly residence.' [1]

Suburbia also finds expression in these few words—

> Villas with the titles of royalty and bloody battles claimed five feet of garden . . [2]

It is a very pleasant, idealistic, and mysterious custom.

Nor should we fail to mention here the story of the 'painful, partially inexcusable, incurable, sense of humour' of Mrs Lupin, and the terrible power Mrs Chump wielded over her.[3]

There is something humorous in the exact reproduction of what is really typical about anybody. For example, if you were talking to a curate and he were suddenly to make a remark or act a gesture just like what you have always supposed a curate should do, you would probably laugh outright in a way that would shock him very much. For it is not necessary to suppose that the curate should do anything particularly silly or unusual, but merely something which seemed to your mind peculiarly typical of curates in general.

[1] *The Case of General Ople and Lady Camper*, chap. i.
[2] *The House on the Beach*, chap. i.
[3] *Sandra Belloni*, chap. xxvii.

Here is a sentence of Meredith's that gives us the precise feeling of this—

...and he though he spoke of insubordination, merited chastisement, and other usher phrases, seemed to melt, and I had what I believe was a primary conception of the power of woman.[1]

Meredith has a great delight in poking fun at people and of making rather dry comments upon solemn occurrences. He is fond of conjuring up the mental attributes of popular customs and of playfully imagining interpretations of the spirit of beer and other thoroughly British institutions—

There is no instrument the sound of which proclaims such vast internal satisfaction as the drum. I know not whether it be that the sense we have of the corpulency of this instrument predisposes us to imagine it supremely content, as when an alderman is heard snoring the world is assured that it listens to the voice of his own exceeding gratulation. A light heart in a fat body ravishes not only the world but the philosopher.[2]

and in the same book comes a sly touch in the shape of a practical illustration of this theory as to its influence—

'That makes a nation strong. Look at England.'
Mr. Barrett observed him stand out largely, as if filled by the spirit of the big drum.[3]

---

[1] *The Adventures of Harry Richmond*, chap. v.
[2] *Sandra Belloni*, chap. ix.
[3] *Sandra Belloni*, chap. viii.

These are all very good instances of his perception of the absurd and humorous in everyday life. They show an eminently valuable thing, namely that he has not lost touch with life such as it is, and is still able to relish these small points, to be oblivious to which may so often mean to be oblivious to far more important realities. Very intellectual people run a grave danger of failing to sympathise with the profound unintellectuality of people in general. They simply cannot comprehend the value people place on small things, and therefore they simply cannot comprehend the people themselves. As I said before, the lesson of humour is the lesson of the practical equality of everyone. Perhaps one of the greatest things about it is just the very fact that it is not an intellectual gift but very truly a gift meant for all. I need not repeat that it is democratic and universal. Many do not know and never could know what it means, but in proportion there are not improbably amongst such as many patricians as porters.

To see with clear eyes what is humorous in life betokens a sense far wider than the one obviously apparent. It shows that essential sanity which is the balance of society, and it shows an inherent grasp of the foundations of equality.

When you are put to explain any abstract word, you are apt to do so entirely from its positive standpoint. But a word like humour has roots beneath as well as above the surface. It not only means a definite thing in itself but leavens and modifies the meanings of many other things. For instance, a distinct lack of humour in application to art would probably result at some time or other in a sudden horrible hiatus of judgment or power. For humour is to some degree the atmosphere that surrounds all phases of life. In the very happiness of its heart it speaks of the elemental joyfulness of existence, and is one of the strongest arguments against the pessimists.

Humour is more apparent in Meredith's earlier works than in his later ones. *The Shaving of Shagpat* and *Evan Harrington* are founded in humour and built upon a broad basis of it. In the later works it tends to become merged in the finer analysis of comedy, though everywhere there are flashes of its negative and positive lights.

The laughter of humour is herculean but by no means boorish. Nothing could be less humorous than mental buffoonery as such, and in nothing is the line of demarcation betwixt the true and the false more subtle and yet more complete. Meredith has most happily expressed its philosophic meaning in some lines of his first sonnet on Shakespeare—

> . . . thence had he the laugh
> We feel is thine [1]: broad as ten thousand beeves
> At pasture! [2]

This is the deep sense of humour that can mark through all the desperate failures of life that inherent root of sanity and brotherhood which is the very pith and structure of life. Humour is at the heart of true optimism. A belief in tangible progress requires some belief in things as they are, for otherwise there could be no foundation to build upon ; and of all things, humour teaches (perhaps more clearly than anything else teaches it) the good that does underlie much of the sham and cruelty of civilization.

[1] thine=nature's.
[2] *The Spirit of Shakespeare*, i.

CHAPTER XIII

Aphorist and Metaphorist

GEORGE MEREDITH has always been famous as an aphorist, for was it not in *Richard Feverel* that 'The Pilgrim's Scrip' first shed into the light the flashes of his ironical and cryptic wit. And ever since then he has used it as a mouthpiece for expounding his philosophy of society. The aphorism appears to him an impersonal method of making personal comments upon the world and upon life in general. It sums up in one sentence a whole mental position and is the gateway to a field of reflection. It is in fact the thoughtful essence of passing ideas and the piercing flash that searches out the heart of a subject. Aphorisms need not be too apparent but they must contain only the pith. They must be vital in their truth and significance. Nothing could have less point than an aphorism that was pointless, and no surer method of exposing incompetency could be suggested than the making of aphorisms that were without direct application. It would show little but a complacent conceit. And so the aphorist has to be not only a brilliant but a sound thinker, not only a wit but a philosopher. Anyone who has read Meredith's works must have seen that his is a mind peculiarly suitable to the growth of aphorisms. Its whole equipment is that of a self-conscious and deep thinker who has a mastery over the eloquent in language and expression. For the aphorism, to bear full fruit, must be a literary production and hit the mark not merely from its truth but from the exquisite delicacy with which the truth is advanced. Our ideas are only visible to outsiders through the medium of words and the cultivation of language brightens the spark of perception.

Chapters in this book have been devoted to comedy and humour, and this one might almost have been called a chapter on wit. For the aphorism is essentially a witty saying, though it is weighted with more seriousness than is necessary to the chance thrusts of the recognized wit. Indeed the wit tries simply to shine outwardly whereas the aphorist endeavours also to illumine the mind. In fact, the aphorism is one of the barbs of thought, and it strikes a sudden and awakening blow by the very force of concentration. I will use a quotation from Meredith to describe what is its real method—

> Clara communicated as much as she was able in one of those looks of still depth which say, Think! and without causing a thought to stir, take us into the pellucid mind.[1]

I have said before in this book that Meredith is a man keenly aware of the real power of language. That is one of the main reasons of his success as an aphorist. For the further the aphorism recedes from the hackneyed both in thought and in interpretation of thought, the more remarkable will it be. For instance, this quotation is quite sound in its truth but it is not very orginial or suggestive, and consequently it cannot be said to be particularly striking—

> When we appear most incongruous, we are often exposing the key to our characters . .[2]

but this one is on a totally different level—

> . . . criticism is the end of worship; the Brutus blow at that Imperial but mortal bosom . .[3]

---

[1] *The Egoist*, chap. xliii.
[2] *Rhoda Fleming*, chap. xix.
[3] *Lord Ormont and His Aminta*, chap. ix.

APHORIST AND METAPHORIST

Here the idea literally springs before us, admirable both in conception and phraseology. I give below a few examples of this fresh and masterly handling of themes, that are old because they are universal, and new because they are the problems that every man and woman comes in contact with —

Who rises from Prayer a better man, his prayer is answered.[1]

Slight exaggerations do more harm to truth than reckless violations of it.[2]

For this reason so many fall from God, who have attained to Him; that they cling to Him with their Weakness, not with their Strength.[3]

In action, Wisdom goes by majorities.[4]

Meredith has seen that the human mind is extraordinarily susceptible to impression if only it can be made in a vivid, unique, and immediate manner. It takes thought rather like it takes medicine—in quick, sharp doses. His aphorisms captivate the intelligence through these very qualities. They strike at the root and avoid side issues. They are strong, but

---

[1] *The Ordeal of Richard Feverel*, chap. xii.
[2] *The Case of General Ople and Lady Camper*, chap. viii.
[3] *The Ordeal of Richard Feverel*, chap. xxii.
[4] *The Ordeal of Richard Feverel*, chap. i.

the strength is used and the blow finished, in a moment. The mind is not kept at a high tension in considering them, for their true power lies in the fact that they are like springs, that are unwound by the machinery of the brain, till through the kaleidoscope of changes, it too grasps in a flash the message of the whole. When he makes a remark like this—

> Nonsense of enthusiasts is very different from nonsense of ninnies.[1]

or like this—

> . . . . there is more in the world than the epigrams aimed at it contain.[2]

we feel that we can, so to speak, digest them in quiet to get their absolute distinction, though directly they are uttered, some sense of their meaning is quite apparent.

And what indeed could be wiser than some of these aphorisms. Take the following—

> The compensation for Injustice, is, that in that dark Ordeal we gather the worthiest around us.[3]

---

[1] *The Ordeal of Richard Feverel,* chap. xlii.
[2] *The Tragic Comedians,* chap. viii.
[3] *The Ordeal of Richard Feverel,* chap. i.

APHORIST AND METAPHORIST

In all cases where two have joined to commit an offence, punish one of the two lightly.[1]

When nations gain the pitch where rhetoric
Seems reason, they are ripe for cannon's food.[2]

They are the outcome of a philosophic wisdom that has looked at life not indeed without bitter things to remember and gloomy memories of darkness, but still with that sure and calm vision which rises at last out of despair and grief and knows that existence is a fight where with strength and preparedness the down-trodden will at length become the conquerors and the hopeless workers gain the rest they have been looking for. Does he not himself say—

There is for the mind but one grasp of happiness: from that uppermost pinnacle of wisdom whence we see that this world is well designed.[3]

The aphorism is one of the most self-conscious of literary productions, and Meredith is perhaps the most self-conscious of aphorists. I do not mean that it is a small self-consciousness, for indeed it might well be called the reverse. Self-consciousness is, in this aspect, a sort of crucible into which the rough ore of

[1] *The Ordeal of Richard Feverel*, chap. xxvii.
[2] *On the Danger of War.*
[3] *The Ordeal of Richard Feverel*, chap. x.

thoughts and words are poured, and from which comes forth the refined essence of both, harmoniously and beautifully blended. For the aphorism is the polished alloy of the intellect and the imagination. The intellect conceives a situation of commanding interest and the imagination sets to work to convey an impression of it all brilliant and rounded as is the full moon in the midnight sky. It is easy to notice that Meredith's aphorisms were written in a critical and pondering spirit. It is well-known that ease of expression is the result of a long apprenticeship and it may be presumed that the more apt the aphorism, the more severe the trouble expended. Diligence in practice is essential to a mastery of phrase, and nothing is harder to accomplish than the inevitable word.

It is strange enough that nowadays the newest form of aphorism should take the shape of paradox. There is a kind of fascination about paradoxes that has misled many to consider them the real truth in the guise of twentieth-century parables. To say that a thing is hard because it is easy, or intricate because it is simple, would strike one at first as entirely senseless, but if we look very earnestly into every such remark we shall find that in each of them (more or less) there is a certain amount of truth. The origin of everything is equally obscure and unknowable and therefore everything, in this light, is also equally obscure and unknowable. And thus a thing which appears to our eyes obviously difficult, is really less so, than a thing which appears obviously simple; or rather, we can explain one down to a certain point (or at least imagine an explanation), we cannot at all explain the other. Of course it is true that in the end both reach the same point—a fact however which is not always transparent. Indeed much poring over the innermost applications of paradox will produce mental numbness in the midst of what seems intense mental agility. It is the numbness that has seized powerful minds again and again in the world's sad history—the numbness of mental exaggeration. Is it not only too obvious that the followers of this creed have started upon a circle that can bring them at last to no other point than that whence they started? The way to progress lies along no such line. The true aphorism does not, so to speak, return upon itself, but pierces forward to the core, throwing deeper significance upon the old thoughts under all their modern disguises and making more suggestive the common and therefore unheeded truths of conduct and philosophy. If the aphorism is primarily the appreciation of the value and fitness of condensing language into epigrammatic phrases for the purpose of arousing thought, the metaphor (and in this wide meaning there is no difference between metaphor and simile) is primarily the sense, not so much of awakening, as of charming the mind through poetical imagery and indelible contrasts and likenesses. The maker of metaphors is not necessarily the maker of aphorisms, though there are qualities common to both—George Eliot could make aphorisms, but I do not know that she could make metaphors; Shelley could make metaphors, but I do not know that he could make aphorisms. What is common to both is that strange and complete felicity of language in concentrated form that can cast before the mind's eye the thought of the image. Except Shakespeare, I know of no one more gifted in this double respect than Meredith. Like his command of aphorism, so is his command of metaphor. He has realized the great truth about metaphors, namely that they themselves must have atmosphere and be in them-

APHORIST AND METAPHORIST 267

selves and apart from the thing with which they are compared, a picture. That is to say, they must contain those definite qualities of the aphorism, which make both it and the metaphor very real assets in literature. Take for instance some of those metaphors in which man and nature are set off against one another—

> So she waited, as some grey lake lies, full and smooth, awaiting the star below the twilight.[1]
>
> Surely the eyes of the Chief met the eyes of Bhanavar, as when the brightest stars of midnight are doubled in a clear dark lake.[2]
>
> About her mouth a placid humour slipped
> The dimple, as you see smooth lakes at eve
> Spread melting rings where late a swallow dipped.[3]

How clearly is the actual state of mind shown to us in the descriptions of the inanimate world with which it is compared. It proves that in this sense the metaphor is a cunning instrument of the audible psychologist. It is a means of laying bare the heart in so striking a way, that in the large vagueness of the comparison, a fuller view of it is obtained than in the laborious labyrinths of minute description. The metaphor must indeed be

---

[1] *Sandra Belloni*, chap. xvii.
[2] *The Shaving of Shagpat*, 'The Story of Bhanavar.'
[3] *The Sage enamoured and the Honest Lady*, section i.

268 APHORIST AND METAPHORIST

accurate in this broad method. When Meredith says—

> He was the genius of Champagne luncheon incarnate.[1]
>
> A kiss is but a kiss now ! and no wave
> Of a great flood that whirls me to the sea.[2]
>
> . . . but that Chief dashed forward like a flame beaten level by the wind . .[3]

we grasp a convincing picture of what he intends to convey. The essence of it really does lie in the comparison and does heighten our understanding of what he is comparing it with.

Of course, many metaphors are as aphoristical as metaphorical. They are made up of the spirit of both and couched in language which is the language of either. For example—

> The ladies were scaling Society by the help of the Arts.[4]
>
> . . . the Past lay beside him like a corpse that he had slain.[5]
>
> Solitude is pasturage for a suspicion.[6]

are all proverbs under an obvious modernity, and are spiced with both metaphor and aphorism.

Meredith's fertile brain is constantly brim-

---

[1] *Rhoda Fleming*, chap. xxvii.
[2] *Modern Love*, stanza xxix.
[3] *The Shaving of Shagpat*, ' The Story of Bhanavar.'
[4] *Sandra Belloni*, chap. i.
[5] *Evan Harrington*, chap. xxxix.
[6] *Sandra Belloni*, chap. xxviii.

ming over with thoughts that leap into imagery to find an outlet unhackneyed in form and suitable to a fresh presentation of the eternal subjects. Every mind has a peculiarly personal and unique manner of looking at all the ancient problems of society. Personality in its remote foundations seems governed by no known laws and presents for itself new solutions of problems and apparently fantastical ways of considering life, which perhaps in their entirety can never be grasped by any but that personality. In Meredith's aphorisms and metaphors we see an attempt to present, in a personality of words corresponding to the personality of thought, his view of these questions. A simple idea is for him bathed in a flood of imagery and he tries to make us feel in what way it flashes upon his mind. Personality, perhaps the most profoundly obscure thing in the world, is at the same time perhaps the most profoundly interesting. Language may hint at it and deeds give glimpses of it, but it must remain a mystery for ever, not only to the watcher but the owner. Thus originality and force in presentation of it are essential to any kind of comprehension. Only then can it begin to stand out as the living and vital governor of action.

270 APHORIST AND METAPHORIST

Here, for instance, are expressions of what I refer to—

The blissful minutes rolled away like waves that keep the sunshine out at sea.[1]

Skepsey toned his assent to the diminishing thinness where a suspicion of the negative begins to wind upon a distant horn.[2]

The stroke of Then and Now rang in his breast like a bell instead of a bounding heart.[3]

Gossip must often have been likened to the winged insect bearing pollen to the flowers; it fertilizes many a vacuous reverie.[4]

Rumour blew out a candle and left the wick to smoke in relation to their former intercourse.[5]

At first glance it might seem that he was wrapping up the thought or the idea he wished to convey, but at the second it will be seen that a far more powerful sense of it is carried by the imagery of language than would be true were the case stated in blunt and simple phrases. The fact is that the intelligence has to be wooed, and will in many cases listen only to the voice of the charmer. The metaphorist searches the world for new kingdoms. Nothing in itself need be too bizarre for comparison and nothing indeed too

---

[1] *Vittoria*, chap. xxxvii.
[2] *One of our Conquerors*, chap. iv.
[3] *Beauchamp's Career*, chap. xl.
[4] *Lord Ormont and His Aminta*, chap. vii.
[5] *The Tragic Comedians*, chap. xiii.

commonplace. For the airy filament of the metaphor has above all this function to fulfil— it must be strikingly and convincingly contrasted to the idea of which it is the mirror. I will close this chapter by quoting one more of Meredith's metaphors, one that sums up both in tone and language those brilliant gifts of originality and finesse, which have rightly made him the great modern master of the aphorism and the metaphor—

. . . here she comes, with a romantic tale on her eye-lashes . . [1]

---

[1] *The Egoist*, chap. ii.

CHAPTER XIV
The Eloquence of Meredith

It has become apparent to me, that there is something about Meredith's writings which can only be fully expressed by the word eloquence. I have again and again found myself baffled in trying to grasp through other channels this aspect of his work, and unable to explain a certain tone, which though indefinable was yet palpable. To say concisely what this word conveys would perhaps 'admit a wide solution'. We might call it the thrilling quality of language brought to bear on absorbing subjects, a kind of purified and exalted rhetoric, standing indeed in much the same relation to that as poetry does to prose. Hazlitt in a note to his *Lectures on the English Poets* says 'the difference between poetry and eloquence is that the one is the eloquence of the imagination, and the other of the understanding. Eloquence tries to persuade the will, and convince the reason; poetry produces its effect by instantaneous sympathy.'[1] Though it seems to me

[1] Lecture I, 'On Poetry in General.'

that Hazlitt to some degree confounds eloquence with rhetoric, still his remark, that the appeal is to reason, is very striking. What eloquence describes must in itself have the inherent qualities of eloquence.

To make myself clear in defining the scope of eloquence, and what exactly I mean by it, it will I think serve a useful purpose to give some examples of it from other writers. For instance, the last few sentences of Sir Thomas Browne's *Garden of Cyrus* are in the highest degree eloquent, that is to say, they are filled with a magnetic sway of language and thought. The latter part of chap. xv. of Paul's first *Epistle to the Corinthians*, contains eloquence of a noble sort. Carlyle again can be very eloquent, as in his description of the execution of Marie Antoinette in *The Diamond Necklace*, (chap. vii) and in occasional passages from *Sartor Resartus*, and Ruskin sometimes, as in his description of the 'Slave Ship' in *Modern Painters* (ii. v. 3. xxxix). Victor Hugo, though frequently inclined to be rhetorical, can rise on occasion to supreme flights of eloquence. The last scene between Jean Valjean and the Bishop in *Les Misérables* (book 2, chap xii) is the very heart of it, and the episode of the octopus in *Les Travailleurs de la Mer* (book

4, chaps. i–iii) is not very far inferior to that. Walt Whitman's prose descriptions of night and battles are profoundly eloquent, and in fact his poetry (owing possibly to its peculiar structure) is the same. I have seen a passage of Coleridge's *Anima Poetae* (chap. x) in which he described a bell striking solemnly over sleeping Antwerp in the silence of the night, which was almost unmatched in magnificent eloquence, and Stevenson's picture of night in the open in *Travels with a Donkey*, ('A Night among the Pines') and Hardy's description of the waiting moorland in *The Return of the Native* (chap. i) are of somewhat the same calibre.

I think I need scarcely give further examples to represent my meaning of the word. It is the sort of blend of thought and language which causes one to feel a shiver of some strange and splendid sensation.

It is not easy to apply the test of eloquence to poetry, for then you begin to trespass on the borders of lyricism, which bears strong affinity to it but cannot be said to be the same thing. Nevertheless there are occasions on which the term is applicable. The eloquent moment in poetry is eloquent because it touches upon the very springs of emotion. It is the contrast from something which is in itself transfixing to something else, risen grandly from the earth, ethereal, sublime in itself and sublimer far because it is the climax to a scene already full of meaning. The contrast is complete; from the earthly to the heavenly, from human emotion to a sudden luminous star, from the dead present to living remembrance. We may call it pent-up emotion, leaping free at a tremendous coincidence. The moment must be graphic, kinetic energy of warm water bursting into steam: tragic, because it gives us the glorious thrill starting a tear in the eye. The idea of it runs through great poets. In Shakespeare we see it for instance in *Romeo and Juliet*. It is the night scene. These two are talking in whispers. She entreats him not yet to leave her. From the balcony he sees the first colour of the morning tingeing the cloud above the mountain. Leaning forward he says—

Night's candles are burned out . .[1]

And notice the touch in Fitzgerald's first version of *Omar Khayyam*. The philosopher and Saki are sitting in a darkened garden. All day long he has been expounding to her his philosophy. It is hopeless and it leads to

[1] Act iii. scene v.

nothing. As day closes on them they become quiet and sit thinking and dreaming. The twilight deepens and the stillness deepens. No sound, not even of sighing night breeze, echoes round them; no light, however far or faint, is on them. And as they sit there, all of a sudden they see slowly rising in front of them the large and yellow moon. The Philosopher stretches out his hand—

> Ah, Moon of my Delight who know'st no wane
> The Moon of Heav'n is rising once again . .[1]

And we can observe it in Tennyson's *The Passing of Arthur*. Sir Bedivere, the last of the knights, has seen king Arthur borne away on the barge. He has watched till it has disappeared on the horizon line. All seems over. The sickness of failure is on him. Arthur himself had grown doubtful at the end. He is the last, and he has nothing left to live for, and as he turns sadly away—

> Then from the dawn it seem'd there came, but faint . .

And in Meredith we find an example in *The Ballad of Past Meridian*. The wanderer has met Death, who says to him ominously, 'I gather'. He goes on and meets Life, who murmurs, 'As Thou hast carved me such am

[1] *Omar Khayyám*, edition of 1859, quatrain lxxiv.

I'; and as he thinks of these things, and realizes their cold, truthful fatality—

Then memory, like the nightjar on the pine . .[1]

Such then is the eloquent moment in poetry. It is full of significance and full of splendour; a note that touches the highest and lowest intelligences—simple, direct, terrible, unrealizable. It is melodramatic, without melodrama, and emotional, with no emotion. It is convincing because it is intensely serious, and strong because it is daring.

Eloquence is not common. For one reason it requires a great amount of ability, for another it needs in general a remarkable subject. It would be interesting to trace how far it is an intangible thing, whose spirit might run right through a book, without showing any individual scenes, easily comprehended as such. Perhaps Emily Brontë's *Wuthering Heights* would be the typical example. I seem to see in Meredith's novels this double spirit, though it is far more completely developed as regards individual scenes than as regards the atmosphere of whole works. Certainly the basic plots and philosophy of such books as *Vittoria* and *Richard Feverel* are eloquent, but there is in them such a diversity of action and

[1] Stanza iii.

thought, that the sense of unity and singleness of aim is inclined to become less clear than true eloquence would demand. It is in detached episodes and descriptions that his real sense of eloquence is aroused. Here he concentrates all the forces of language and emotion to set and noble purposes, and forces himself to rise to the level of the theme. So far it is much the same process as the tragic spirit has to pass through, but eloquence is not necessarily tragic; it is simply the great comprehension of great opportunities. The scene in *Vittoria*, where Sandra sings the song of liberty, is a famous instance of Meredith's eloquence. The time was well worthy of the touch of mastery. There was, so to speak, a thrill in the air. How easy it would have been to have over-written his scene or to have failed to grasp its inherent tenseness. Here are Meredith's words—

At the moment of her doing so, Montini whispered in Vittoria's ears. She looked up and beheld the downward curl of the curtain. There was confusion at the wings: Croats were visible to the audience. Carlo Ammiani and Luciano Romara jumped on the stage; a dozen of the noble youths of Milan streamed across the boards to either wing, and caught the curtain desscending. The whole house had risen insurgent with cries of 'Vittoria'! The curtain ropes were in the hands of the Croats, but Carlo, Luciano, and their fellows held the curtain aloft at arm's length at each side of her. She was seen, and she sang, and the house listened.

The Italians present, one and all, rose up reverently and murmured the refrain. Many of the aristocracy would, doubtless, have preferred that this public declaration of the plain enigma should not have rung forth to carry them on the popular current; and some might have sympathized with the insane grin which distorted the features of Antonio Pericles, when he beheld illusion wantonly destroyed, and the opera reduced to be a mere vehicle for a fulmination of politics. But the general enthusiasm was too tremendous to permit of individual protestations. To sit, when the nation was standing, was to be a German. Nor, indeed, was there an Italian in the house who would willingly have consented to see Vittoria silenced, now that she had chosen to defy the Tedeschi from the boards of La Scala. The fascination of her voice extended even over the German division of the audience. They, with the Italians, said, ' Hear her! hear her! ' The curtain was agitated at the wings, but in the centre it was kept above Vittoria's head by the uplifted arms of the twelve young men :—

> 'I cannot count the years,
> That you will drink, like me,
> The cup of blood and tears,
> Ere she to you appears :—
> *Italia, Italia shall be free!*'

So the great name was out, and its enemies had heard it.

> ' You dedicate your lives
> To her, and you will be
> The food on which she thrives,
> Till her great day arrives :—
> *Italia, Italia shall be free!*
> ' She asks you but for faith !
> Your faith in her takes she
> As draughts of heaven's breath,
> Amid defeat and death :—
> *Italia, Italia shall be free!*'

The prima donna was not acting exhaustion when sinking lower in Montini's arms. Her bosom rose and sank quickly, and she gave the terminating verse :—

> 'I enter the black boat
> Upon the wide grey sea.
> Where all her set suns float;
> Thence hear my voice remote :—
> *Italia, Italia shall be free!*'

The curtain dropped.[1]

Indeed *Vittoria* is filled with eloquent passages, as for instance the descriptions of Mazzini,[2] and of the fight between Weisspriess and Angelo Guidescarpi.[3] They are both in a remarkable way compressed and sincere and the language is true to such austere requirements.

Meredith's eloquence springs from a sort of dramatic self-consciousness. He seizes the essential spirit of a scene and fully, grasping what its delineation must demand, braces himself to present with all power the sombre or beautiful ideas that form the instant. He weighs together the language and the thought and brings them into correct association. Many indeed are the eloquent situations that are ruined by the semi-paralysis

---

[1] *Vittoria*, chap. xxi.   [2] chaps. ii and xvii.
[3] chap. xxvi.

of the minds that conceived them. Eloquence may be said to be the absolute balance of words to the most tremendous needs of thought, and the catching of the profound power of any truly dramatic position. Consider for example this quotation from *Sandra Belloni*—

> And sure enough that was the voice of the woods cleaving the night air, not distant. A sleepy fire of early moonlight hung through the dusky fir-branches. The voice had the woods to itself, and seemed to fill them and soar over them, it was so full and rich, so light and sweet. And now, to add to the marvel, they heard a harp accompaniment, the strings being faintly touched, but with firm fingers. A woman's voice; on that could be no dispute. Tell me, what opens heaven more flamingly to heart and mind, than the voice of a woman, pouring clear accordant notes to the blue night sky that grows light blue to the moon? There was no flourish in her singing. All the notes were firm and rounded, and sovereignly distinct. She seemed to have caught the ear of Night, and sang confident of her charm. It was a grand old Italian air, requiring severity of tone and power. Now into great mournful hollows the voice sank steadfastly. One soft sweep of the strings succeeded a deep final note, and the hearers breathed freely.[1]

We can conjure up well enough what would be the feelings all this would arouse and can see how inherently dramatic the moment would be. To write of it just such a touch

[1] Chap. ii.

of eloquence was needed, ringing into our ears the splendid cadence of that forest picture. It is the graphic and deep realization of the inner spirit of romance in this description which compels admiration. I should like to give here another instance of this great ability to catch the essence of a scene of acute emotion—

. . . Rose stood up and hurried round the table to Mrs Strike, who was seen to rise from her chair ; and as she did so, the ill-arranged locks fell from their unnatural restraint down over her shoulders ; one great curl half forward to the bosom, and one behind her right ear. Her eyes were wide, her whole face, neck and fingers, white as marble. The faintest tremor of a frown on her brows, and her shut lips, marked the continuation of some internal struggle, as if with her last conscious force she kept down a flood of tears and a wild outcry which it was death to hold.[1]

As I said above, eloquence is closely allied to lyricism ; or rather you must have lyricism in eloquence, though you need not have eloquence in lyricism. As to its relationship to rhetoric ; where they do treat of the same subject, the contrast is between a highly artistic and a highly inartistic handling, but very frequently, the things dealt with by each revolve in entirely different spheres. For indeed eloquence can to some extent be worked into quite simple things, but the basis of most

[1] *Evan Harrington*, chap. xxii.

THE ELOQUENCE OF MEREDITH

rhetoric is pomposity. This vignette of a girl is as beautiful as it is eloquent—

> She was bright as the sunset gardens of the Golden Apples. The braids of her yellow hair were bound in wreaths, and on one side of her head a saffron crocus was stuck with the bell downwards. Sweetness, song and wit hung like dews of morning on her grape-stained lips.[1]

and here is another eloquent portrait, even though it may have in it a touch of cruelty—

> Her hair was radiant in a shady street; her eyelids tenderly toned round the almond enclosure of blue pebbles, bright as if shining from the seawash. The lips of the fair woman could be seen to say that they were sweet when, laughing or discoursing, they gave sight of teeth proudly her own, rivalling the regularity of the grin of dentistry. A Venus of nature was melting into a Venus of art, and there was a decorous concealment of the contest and the anguish in the process, for which Lord Ormont liked her well enough to wink benevolently at her efforts to cheat the world at various issues, and maintain her duel with Time.[2]

The sense of eloquence almost more than any other is a stronghold to the novelist. It gives him a feeling of power and enables him to face any situation with a calm hope of grappling successfully with its possibilities.

---

[1] *Farina*, 'The White Rose Club.'
[2] *Lord Ormont and his Aminta*, chap. xii.

284 THE ELOQUENCE OF MEREDITH

It is the assurance of eloquence that nerves the mind to overcome the difficulties of its own creation and rule the kingdom of the imagination. As Meredith himself says (I have also quoted the sentence elsewhere)—

> A profound belief in the efficacy of his eloquence, when he chose to expend it, was one of the principal supports of Edward's sense of mastery;—a secret sense belonging to certain men in every station of life, and which is the staff of many an otherwise impressible and fluctuating intellect.[1]

It is much the same whether applied to life or literature.

There is, too, an aspect of eloquence which is not particularly touched upon by the short quotation, and at the same time hardly falls into the section which is comprised by the eloquence of the whole plan of a book. I mean that kind of eloquence which teaches of the delight of actual achievement, which glories in the long sustained fights of minorities against majorities. You will notice in many of Meredith's novels the desperate encounters on the social battle-field between the forces of the aspiring and the forces of the great ones. Such comedy has the substance of an eloquence that is distinctly

[1] *Rhoda Fleming*, chap. xxxvii.

remarkable. The way the Harringtons[1] succeed in taking the enemies' citadel and actually living there is one instance. With what joy does Meredith seem to see each victory, and for how long does he allow them to sustain the fray against the fearful odds of suspicious youths. Again the whole story of Richmond Roy [2] is a chapter in the history of eloquent resistance. Meredith lingers on his victories and makes us wish that he might win the impossible battle. Take still another instance, that of Lord Romfrey's apology to Dr Shrapnel.[3] How protracted and thrilling is the encounter between uncle and nephew, and how eloquent is the imagination involved. And once again, remember the story of Alvan and Clothilde von Rüdiger [4]; does he not almost succeed in his desperate effort? The stories of Sir Willoughby Patterne and Clara Middleton,[5] of Victor Radnor [6] and his position in society, and numerous others, might also be cited. Meredith seems to have been the first man (unless we make an exception

[1] *Evan Harrington.*
[2] *The Adventures of Harry Richmond.*
[3] *Beauchamp's Career.*
[4] *The Tragic Comedians.*
[5] *The Egoist.*
[6] *One of our Conquerors.*

of Cervantes with the episode in *Don Quixote* of Sancho Panza's governorship of ' the Island of Barataria '[1], and of Shakespeare with the whole story of Sir John Falstaff in both parts of *King Henry IV*.) to have properly understood the eloquence of these drawn-out battles, to have grasped the invigorating sensation of the keen encounters of mind and mind, to have seen dramatic possibilities of such a description in the opposition of fiery and stubborn wills.

The touch of eloquence is a touch that to a considerable extent underlies the whole nature of an eloquent writer. It is the capability of seizing from its most salient standpoint an episode or period of distinction, and yet it is something more than that. It is in fact the perception of the greatness and romance of great and romantic things. Such a statement may appear to have little force or meaning, but I do not think that it is so. There are an endless number of persons quite incapable of grasping the deep and dramatic eloquence of life, and it is amazing with what platitudes the terrible moments of life and death are faced by innumerable people. Surely existence is one panorama of culmin-

[1] Part ii, chap. xlv *et seq.*

THE ELOQUENCE OF MEREDITH

ating and frightful eloquence. There is nothing unimportant in the world, and philosophy looks gravely both at stars and starlings. The complete mystery of consciousness is an overwhelming example of the eloquence of silence. Everywhere there is a breathless waiting for a sentence that will never be pronounced and for an answer that will never be given. Meredith is one of those great men that have taken a truly eloquent view of life, and have been enabled by their genius to convey this eloquence in writing. How many people there are whose minds think nothing but the most trivial thoughts on even the profoundest subjects. Eloquence is indeed the dawn of power, the beginning of aspiration.

CHAPTER XV

Last Words on Criticism, Method and some Omissions

It must be obvious to any one who has read this book that the last thing it could properly be called would be a criticism. The truth is, there is little of the critical method in it. If anything it is an interpretation of certain striking features in Meredith's works as seen through the eyes of one as anxious after the ideal as the actual accomplishment. For I must candidly admit that I may on occasions have read into Meredith's words, thoughts that may not have been his, or at any rate not his with that especial element in them, in which has lain their ultimate value for me.[1] Had the intention been to produce a criticism, such a statement would be altogether fatal, but as the case stands, I do not feel

---

[1] Perhaps the second part of the general introduction contains as representative an example of this as may be found. To Meredith the philosophic aspect of his poetry is probably more important than the lyric, but I have dwelt almost entirely on the latter as being of far more absorbing interest to myself.

altogether so guilty as might be supposed. For, after all, the worth of a book lies largely in the sensation it gives its reader, and its power is not only in its own philosophy but in its influence upon the world. And certainly these are two things which may not run in the same groove. It is conceivable that the tragedy of Richard Feverel might not affect a person, whereas the writing in which the tragedy is evolved might deeply affect him. This is a very simple example of what I refer to, but I should like to give another, which is really much nearer the truth of my own case. Let us say that a man is a profound admirer of Shelley or Walt Whitman or Turgenieff. They are writers whose inherent philosophies and personalities are in many respects utterly unlike those of George Meredith, and yet in Meredith will be found much noble writing strangely harmonious to the real minds of all three. Well, it is possible to read an author mainly from the point of view of another author, and mainly to gain from him still further beautiful ideas along the lines of that other author's grasp of life and poetry. Such a reading need by no means miss the salient and true features of a writer, but on occasions, where his mind does seem to approximate to that of the other's, there will very probably creep into the reader's judgment a distortion of what is his actual meaning. He will become not the critic of what he is reading, but the envoy of the writer he so much admires. He will be constantly comparing him to the ideal another would have had before him on such an occasion, and perhaps even strain the words to fit a meaning he earnestly desires them to be fulfilling. And carrying this idea one step further it must be apparent that a certain trend of mind might very well read an author mainly for the purpose of magnifying and illustrating that special trend; the poetical would ignore all but the poetical, the philosophical all but the philosophical, and in fact, personality seek illustration of itself in the personality of another.

This explanation may in part define the scope of the work, but I should like to add one more which ought to make the position still clearer. The book, as I say, is frankly an interpretation—an exegesis. And this being allowed, I have seldom tried to interpolate words of dispraise. The idea was to expound what was of value, why it was of value, and of what great value it was in itself, quite apart from drawbacks, the full description of which might have lessened the force of the remarks. For those things I have mentioned as being remarkable, actually are remarkable in themselves, and consequently have been described on their own merits. There are other things which I think are actually not of value in themselves, harmful very likely, but I have simply ignored them, as outside the scheme of the book. I have certainly now and then touched upon some of them where it was necessary to review a whole position, but, as may be seen, I have done so only to a small extent. This then has been the main plan of the book, a plan, I allow, which lays itself open to attack on a great many different grounds. And even from my own point of view, I am far from supposing that I have exhausted the ore of the mine. It is indeed probable that I have not even understood much of what Meredith teaches, and it is certain that I am not capable of expressing many of his phases. Nor have I tried to do more than write about some of those features which have struck me as of exceptional interest. I am perfectly aware that there are other things I could have enlarged upon, but then, as I again remark, I did not set out to do more than I have tried to do. The scientific criticism of Meredith has yet to be written: probably the time is not yet. The modern spirit he embodies rouses rather the desire to expound, and is inclined to ignore the historic function of criticism. There is of course that very dull thing, which, parading as criticism, is little more than literary history (and generally not nearly as valuable as that), but there is also the school which tries definitely to place an author in the light of universal literature. This is what I refer to, when I say that the scientific spirit of criticism is still non-existent as applied to Meredith.[1]

Even in scientific criticism it is almost impossible to differentiate between a man's greatness as a genius and a man's greatness as a pioneer. For first of all we have to remember that genius itself is subject to its age and may well enough be outside the scope of another age's analysis; and secondly, that the pioneer is indirectly the author of all the pioneers. The nearer a man is to our

[1] An exception to this statement must, however, be made in favour of an article in the *Fortnightly Review* for Dec. 1907, by Mr Laurie Magnus, who explains with admirable knowledge and insight Meredith's logical succession in the roll of XIXth century poetry.

own time, the harder is it to gauge his true perspective. Moreover the field was infinitely narrower long ago, and the chance of recognition consequently larger. If the *Confessio Amantis* were published for the first time to-day in modern English no one would read it, but Gower has a distinct niche in literature : the minor Caroline poets were by no means so poetical as the minor poets of to-day, but the former get into literary histories, while the latter cannot even get into bookshops. Meredith's exact position in the history and the genius of literature is a question that cannot be settled till many years have passed, and the personality of the author has become finally merged in that of his works. Personally, I prefer to hear what a writer actually means to a man, that is to say, what influence one mind has had upon another, and how that influence has worked, but then so many people are not interested in this (and very often, very naturally, I must admit) that one cannot be surprised if it is not the method adopted by the sages.

As to the large use made of quotations throughout the work, I may mention that there seems to me a kind of loss and gain by such a method of presenting an author.

The gain consists, in the case of Meredith, firstly in the extraordinary adaptability of his work to quotation, secondly, in the value of proving your opinions through the mouth of the author. This last is peculiarly true in a book of this description, where the exuberance of praise would be apt to carry along with it even less than the usual modified amount of weight generally allowed to this kind of writing, unless it were backed up by the powerful and arresting language of the author himself. I do not mean that what I say is necessarily proved by the quotations, I do mean that these quotations prove a man of genius. The loss arises, firstly, from a possibly false idea of Meredith being gathered from the given quotations, owing to the fact that as I have wanted to lay special stress on certain features it is more than likely that I shall have chosen quotations suitably representing these phases (and how easy it is to find in the whole life-work of a man chance remarks to endorse almost any opinion), and have ignored others that might have shown a man of entirely different outlook ; and secondly, from the fact that quotations often merely distract the attention of the reader without being in themselves capable of explaining the real spirit of an author. I must own that I chose to give them mainly from the fact of their intrinsic beauty and force. There is scarcely another author who so sparkles in individual sentences and lines of poetry and passion. It is, as I said before, the outcome of a keenly self-conscious mind, fully aware of the power of impressive writing and constantly alert to the opportunity of eloquence of every description. And again, you must remember that I had to write about a man whose works are well-known only by name. If I had written a book about Shakespeare or Milton it would not have been necessary to quote to the same extent, but merely to have mentioned such and such a line or passage as an example of my meaning. I should have assumed, and I think legitimately, that they were already known, but it would be stupid to assume any such knowledge in the case of Meredith. To be at all believed, it was necessary to give signs. Every one had to be taken to be a sort of Didymus. For you can at once discount the influence of ecstatic remarks about unknown things.

Now, though I have expressly stated that this is in no real sense a criticism, I think it would be as well if I enumerated what seem to me the weaker points in the Meredithian method and style. And it must be noted first of all, that in Meredith, as indeed in all writers of strong and distinctive personality, many faults exist purely as the result of merits. Take for instance the subject of obscurity both of thought and language which is a common point of contention. I cannot deny that there is much truth in this, and that, in some of his very latest work, it really does outweigh any corresponding value, but all the same, we must bear in mind that he treats of psychological points which do inherently demand an elusive method of unravelling. Mr Chesterton in his *Robert Browning*, page 156, has the following remarks, 'The works of George Meredith are, as it were, obscure even when we know what they mean. They deal with nameless emotions, fugitive sensations, sub-conscious certainties and uncertainties, and it really requires a somewhat curious and unfamiliar mode of speech to indicate the presence of these'; and Meredith himself once wrote to a correspondent, 'Thought is tough and dealing with thought produces toughness'. The real fault, if I may say so, lies in the fact that he has allowed these things to grow upon him till at last (I speak

METHOD, AND SOME OMISSIONS

mainly of the latest poems—though indeed it is true of many of them) a real nemesis of obscurity has shrouded the gleam of fire.

Again, his plan of describing types has led to some remark against the reality of his creations. For instance, I have heard it said, that when he draws one of his characteristic women he heaps upon her every virtue and noble quality imaginable. As before, there is truth in the statement, but, as before, the fault springs from a virtue of profound significance, the virtue, that is to say, of having conceived the vivid reality of the ideal and the philosophic type. It would however be perhaps true to say that he has more insight into what forms and influences personality than he has into personality itself. The reality of his people suffers considerably from the very analysis he subjects them to and of which he shows them in the throes.

The cryptic qualities of Meredith's style are to some extent signs of a brain in love with its own subtlety. Not seldom he fatigues as much as he exhilarates. His fireworks are at times little more than an inward soliloquy upon ordinary affairs and are quite incomprehensible to the outsider. There is in fact about his work an extreme self-consciousness that can scarcely permit the personality of the author to fall into the background.

There is, too, on occasion an over-elaboration and a note of philosophical didacticism which is not altogether pleasing. Certainly his scheme of both novel-writing and poetry includes philosophy as its basis, but I think it is a striking artistic error to make the lesson too obvious or too laboured. It may be taken as a sound theory that in an artistic production, art should be the first thing aimed at, for without art no principle will carry conviction. The detachment of a Flaubert, a De Maupassant, a Turgenieff, is sign of a temperament keenly aware of the artistic unity demanded by the novel. It is not hard to imagine their shudder at much hint of the personal note. To them the development of the subject, the psychological unravelling of character, the minute search into motive, the ceaseless and unwearied perfection of style, is the aim of art. The obtrusion of themselves is a thing altogether outside any plan of finish or of distinction.

There are naturally a number of alleged faults which are of a controversial character, as, for example, his constant strain after intellectual effect, his perpetual harping on the comic spirit, his stoical philosophy of nature, his frequent improbability of plot, eccentricity of characterization, etc., etc. The judgment on these points is largely a matter of temperament, but on the whole it is probably true that the nearer simplicity is reached, the greater will be the influence in the long run. Personality will fade in years to come and force alone survive into the future. The very fineness of Meredith's mind may weigh against his fame. We live now in an age of nuance and allusion, when life is strangely nerved to a thousand cadences of perception, but it is not altogether unlikely that the future may see in much of this particular growth, merely a phase of society; and in the describer of it, not much more than a local and historical importance. This will not destroy Meredith, for, as I said before, when he has to deal with great crises, he mounts with the theme, in self-control, simplicity and strength, but it will inevitably lessen his general influence. It may be, of course, that the world will continue for centuries along the same line of development, and if such should be the case he will indeed be honoured as a pioneer and supreme master.

Meredith, like everyone else, has had his failures. Of his novels I should myself say that *Rhoda Fleming*, *The Tragic Comedians*, *Diana of the Crossways*, *Lord Ormont and his Aminta* and *The Amazing Marriage* are distinctly poorer than the rest. This, of course, is in comparison with his own works, for certainly even these are most remarkable and able books. Of his poems, as I have several times remarked, the last two volumes, *Odes in Contribution to the Songs of French History*, and *A Reading of Life*, are extremely involved, and many other poems scattered throughout various volumes share an identical fate. His faults of this kind are accentuated to a great degree in his poetry, which, when obscure, is as far as I am concerned, simply impossible of comprehension. I am quite prepared to hear that it is disgraceful of me to admit any such thing, but it is so—and I am not alone.

Of his characters, quite a considerable number are unconvincing, some wholly unreal. I believe, for instance, that Mrs Chump has tried the credibility of many, and I hold no particular brief for Anthony Hackbut or for a good number more. Nor does his style always reflect the light of his mind; I do not necessarily mean in clarity, but in actual capability of expression.

But it is a thankless business to speak of faults, which, after all, mainly arise from striking qualities. I am quite sure that there are more that I could mention, but I am quite sure they are largely the outcome of a powerful mind's individuality. For at heart Meredith is essentially sane and filled with the great and eternal thoughts. The engine of personality works upon the material of life and gives us pictures coloured with its own dyes. We have to realize this in estimating the status of a writer.

I do not suppose there are in this world two more sublime sights than the sky inlaid deeply with stars and the day rising through the mists of the darkness, and I do not suppose there are more beautiful and sublime ideas than these can give us. The final test of things seems to me the test of night and sunrise, and though beneath them we have strange thoughts, still they are simple, uncomplicated, elemental. Here then we may not unnaturally suppose literature must come to its final reckoning, and this the frame of mind that is to judge the work of all the ages. I believe that Meredith will come through such an ordeal into the light of true recognition because he has greatly grasped the great and stirring things of life and poetry and nature. It is not by any means altogether unfitting that those very words he applied to Shakespeare should themselves be applied to him—

Thy greatest knew thee, Mother Earth; unsoured
He knew thy sons. He probed from hell to hell
Of human passions, but of love deflowered
His wisdom was not, for he knew thee well.[1]

---

[1] *Th Spirit of Shakespeare*, i.

INDEX

Adventures of Harry Richmond, The, quoted, 99, 101, 198, 254
Amazing Marriage, The, quoted, 101, 122
Aphorism, 258 *et seq.*; and wit, difference between, 259
Ask, is Love Divine, quoted, 199
Atmosphere, 22, 30, 69, 96

Beauchamp's Career, quoted, 85, 92, 125, 132, 179, 219, 270
Brontë, Emily, 277
Browne, Sir Thomas, 273
Browning, Robert, 60, 190
By Morning Twilight, quoted, 210

Caliban, 218
Carlyle, Thomas, 138, 273
Caroline poets, Minor, and the minor poets of to-day, 293
Carroll, Lewis, 245
Case of General Ople and Lady Camper, The, quoted, 252, 261
Cervantes, Miguel de, 286
Character, 119 *et seq.*
Characters in Meredith's books referred to (apart from those mentioned in quotations); Almeryl, 207; Alvan, 178, 191; Ammiani, Carlo, 154; Asper, Constance, 44, 135; Barret, Sir Purcell, 178, 225; Beauchamp, Nevil, 75, 137, 138–142, 178–181, 190; Belloni, Sandra, 75, 91, 129, 137, 147–154, 170, 278; Bhanavar, 207; Blancove, Edward, 225; Bonner, Juliana, 171; Busche, Lady, 241; Chloe, 171; Chump, Mrs., 253, 300; Crefeldt, Baroness von, 132; Croisnel, Renée de, 75; Culling, Mrs., 132, 170; Culmer, Lady, 241; Dacier, Hon. Percy, 44, 157, 159, 160; Dale, Lætitia, 143, 144, 146–147; Dannisburgh, Lord, 156, 157, 190; Denham, Jenny, 130; Desborough, Lucy, 174, 177, 178, 190, 202–206; Dunstane, Lady, 155, 156, 158; Dunstane, Sir Lukin, 225; Durance, Colney, 178; Eglett, Lady Charlotte

133; Farrell, Aminta, 76; Feverel, Richard, 75, 174–177, 202–206; Feverel, Sir Austin, 125, 174, 175, 225; Fenellan, Simeon, 244; Fleetwood, Lord, 126, 178, 225; Fleming, Dahlia, 172; Fleming, Rhoda, 170; Forey, Clare, 171; Gammon, Master, 247, 248; Gosstre, Lady, 132, 239, 241; Guidascarpi, Angelo, 169, 280; Guidascarpi, Rinaldo, 167, 168, 169; Hackbut, Anthony, 300; Hedger, Andrew, 248–250; Jenkinson, Mrs. Mountstuart, 132, 241; Jocelyn, Lady, 132; Lupin, Mrs., 253; Merion, Dan, 155; Middleton, Clara 143, 145, 146, 285; Ormont, Lord, 125, 178; Patterne, Sir Willoughby, 125, 137, 142–147, 178, 225, 226, 227, 285; Pericles, Antonio, 148, 149; Pole, Mr. 150; Pole, Wilfrid, 148, 149, 150, 151, 178, 223, 224, 225, 227; Poles, Three Miss, 135, 148, 225, 239; Powys, Merthyr, 129, 151, 154; Radnor, Mrs. Victor, 132, 169, 170, 190; Radnor, Nesta, 130, 170; Radnor, Victor, 125, 170, 178, 225, 285; Redworth, Tom, 129, 160; Richmond, Roy, 137, 178, 285; Rizzo, Barto, 153; Romfrey, Lord, 285; Rüdiger, Clotide von, 285; Saldar, Countess de, 135, 239; Shrapnel, Dr. 75, 140, 285; 'Speed-the-Plough,' 250; Sumfit, Mrs., 247; Thresher, John, 251; Tinker in *Richard Feverel*, 250; Tramp in *The Egoist*, 251; Vittoria, see Belloni, Sandra; Warwick, Diana, 137, 154–161, 170; Warwick, Mr., 44, 155, 156, 158; Wathin, Lady, 44, 135; Weisspriess, Captain, 280; Weyburn, Matey, 76, 129; Whitford, Vernon, 129; Wife of Barto Rizzio, 167–169.

Chesterton, Mr. G. K., 161 (quoted), 296 (quoted)
Coleridge, Samuel Taylor, 274
Comedy, 229 *et seq.*; and humour, difference between, 243
Criticism, Difference between exegetical and ordinary, 27 *et seq.*

Dante, 93
Day of the Daughter of Hades, The, quoted, 68
Death, 184 *et seq.*; capable of exalted artistic treatment, 185; holds the

INDEX

keys of memory, 193; its look of nobility, 195
Diana of the Crossways, quoted, 84, 112, 124, 155, 190, 200, 249, 250
Dickens, Charles, 38
Dirge in Woods, quoted, 74

Earth and a Wedded Woman, quoted, 21, 71
Earth's Secret, quoted, 73
Edgar, Professor Pelham, 225 (quoted)
Egoism and Sentimentalism, 218 *et seq.*
Egoist, The, quoted, 125, 134, 144, 145, 217, 223, 236, 237, 244, 260, 271
Eliot, George, 266
Eloquence, 272 *et seq.*; some examples of, from other writers, 273; in poetry, 275; of life, 286
Essay on Comedy, quoted, 229, 230, 231, 232
Evan Harrington, quoted, 91, 172, 268, 282

Farina, quoted, 47, 283
Finity and infinity, 187
Fitzgerald, Edward, 275
Flaubert, Gustave, 54 *n.* 298

Gower, John, 293
Grandfather Bridgeman, quoted, 97
Greatness, Universal affinity to, 55
Greek sculpture, 8

Harcourt, Sir William, 244
Hardy, Thomas, 274
Hazlitt, William, 272 (quoted)
Henderson, Mrs. Sturge, 35 (quoted)
House on the Beach, The, quoted, 253
Hugo, Victor, 54 *n.*, 172 (quoted), 273
Humour, 38, 243 *et seq.*, and comedy, difference between, 243
Hymn to Colour, quoted, 62

Ibsen, Henrik, 106, 107
Idealism and realism, 1 *et seq.*
Infinity and finity, 187

Johnson, Samuel, 51

Keats, John, 30

Lamb, Charles, 38
Liberty, Definition of, 23
Literature, Final test of, 301
Lord Ormont and his Aminta, quoted, 102, 133, 244, 260, 270, 283
Love, 197 *et seq.*; definition of, 24; great atmosphere of, 209; tragic emotions of, 212; its melody, 215
Love in the Valley, quoted, 83, 88, 97, 98, 211
Lucifer in Starlight, quoted, 78

INDEX

Magnus, Mr. Laurie, 292 n.
Marie Antoinette, 273
Marriage question, 108 et seq.
Maupassant, Guy de, 298
Mazzini, Giuseppe, 280
Meditation under Stars, quoted, 93
Melampus, quoted, 63
Meredith, George ; type of mind, 30 ; characteristics of, 31 ; self-consciousness of, 32, 42, 263, 280 ; intellectual keenness, 33 ; sense of poetry, 33 ; sense of humour, 34, 247 ; knowledge and love of Nature, 34 ; grasp of his subject, 35 ; to understand him, essential to have read some of his best work, 39 ; an aristocratic radical in mind, 40 ; power of idealization, 41 ; very human in his sympathies, 42 ; stoicism, 43 ; dislike of fools, 43 ; poetical conception of life, 45 ; three periods of his prose works, 47 ; poems not so easily divided into periods, 49 ; style, 51 ; vocabulary, 53 ; cosmic mind, 54 ; significance of nature to, 58 ; type of optimism, 60 ; natural mysticism, 61 ; realization of nature's sanity, 65, 77, 104 ; uses nature to point the metaphor at man, 75 ; love of nature's beauty, 82 ; descriptions of dawn, 83 ; descriptions of night, 86 ; descriptions of the seasons, 96 ; descriptions of mountains, woods, etc., 100 ; comparison with Ibsen, 107 ; belief in society, 108 ; views on marriage, 109 ; views on the position of women, 112 ; attitude towards politics, 114 ; endeavour to make romance a part of life, 115 ; comprehension of justice and liberty, 117 ; poetical light thrown over his characters, 119 ; realizes that character is to be read in niceties, 122 ; aphoristic gift of defining abstract character, 124 ; understands the universal traits, 125 ; creates living figures, 128 ; types that have his sympathy, 128 ; remarkable knowledge of women, 130 ; liking for romantic characters, 137 ; analysis of Nevil Beauchamp, 138 ; analysis of Sir Willoughby Patterne, 142 ; analysis of Sandra Belloni, 147 ; analysis of Diana Warwick, 154 ; secret of his conception of character, 161 ; stand-

INDEX

points from which he surveys life, 162 ; difference between his view of humanity and Walt Whitman's, 163 ; double grasp of tragedy, 166 ; Barto Rizzo's wife, his most tragic figure, 167 ; tragedy of the Brothers Guidascarpi, 169 ; tragedy of Mrs. Victor Radnor, 169 ; tragedy of Chloe, 171 ; *Rhoda Fleming*, a tragic story, 172 ; *Modern Love*, a tragic poem, 173 ; analysis of three tragic figures in *The Ordeal of Richard Feverel*, 174 ; Nevil Beauchamp's death, 178 ; the significance of the tragic to, 182 ; optimism in the face of death, 187 ; dramatic sense of the shock of death, 190 ; dislike of sentimental dwelling on death-scenes, 192 ; final views on actual knowledge, 196 ; his opinion of love, 198 ; lyrical descriptions of love-scenes, 202 ; claims egoism as a universal trait, 216 ; definition of sentimentalism, 218 ; sees impersonalism of egoism, 218 ; sees self-consciousness of sentimentalism, 220 ; some of his typical sentimentalists and egoists, 225 ; sees falseness of the sentimentalist, 226 ; Sir Willoughby Patterne and Wilfred Pole as incurable sentimental egoists, 227 ; sentimentalism, a form of mock sentiment, 228 ; the spirit of comedy in all his work, 229 ; upper classes most suitable for the development of comedy, 230 ; difference between comedy, satire, irony, and humour, 230 ; *Essay on Comedy*, 234 ; difference between his earlier and his later comedy, 235 ; some of the comic situations in his books, 238 ; imaginary difference in describing a humorous event between him and Lewis Carroll, 245 ; not a professedly humorous writer, 247 ; the humour of the soil, 247 ; keenly analytical of the absurd, 252 ; humour more apparent in his earlier than in his later works, 256 ; as aphorist, 258, 269 ; eloquence of, 272, 278 ; delight in long sustained social encounters, 284 ; scientific criticism of, still almost non-existent, 292 ; adaptability of his work to quotation, 294 ; some

INDEX

reasons for his obscurity, 296 ; some faults, 296 ; some alleged faults, 298 ; some of his failures, 300 ; essential sanity of, 301 ; the certainty of his final true recognition, 302

Metaphor, 266 *et seq.*

Milton, John, 93, 295

Minotaur, The, 218

Modern Love, quoted, 89, 97, 100, 116, 173, 194, 196, 268

Molière, Jean Baptiste, 235

Morgue, The, 195

Nature, Two ways of looking at 56, *et seq.* ; her impersonality, 64 ; emotions aroused by, 68 ; her sanity, 75, 78, 104 ; danger of reading our own emotions into, 76 ; her unselfishness, 79

Nature and Life, quoted, 66

Night of Frost in May, quoted, 102

Ode to the Spirit of Earth in Autumn, quoted, 96, 103, 189

On the Danger of War, quoted, 263

One of Our Conquerors, quoted, 6, 85, 170, 189, 212, 270

Optimism, Three different kinds of, in face of the unknown, 60

Orchard and the Heath, The, quoted, 89

Ordeal of Richard Feverel, The, quoted, 65, 89, 102, 123, 132, 133, 175, 177, 203, 204, 206, 221, 250, 261, 262, 263

Outer and Inner, quoted, 80

Pastoral V, quoted, 87

Pastoral VII, quoted, 87

Pater, Walter, 50

Paul, St., 273

Peacock, Thomas Love, 244

Personality, 28 *et seq.* ; rights of, 105 *et seq.*

Poetry, Varying power of comprehension of, 15 *et seq.* ; vocal, must contain art, 19 ; and romance, difference between, 20 ; not primarily didactic, 25 ; eloquence in, 275

Politics, 114

Rabelais, François, 244

Realism and idealism, 1 *et seq.*

Rhoda Fleming, quoted, 124, 126, 127, 131, 172, 173, 228, 248, 260, 268, 284

Ruskin, John, 273

Sage Enamoured and the Honest Lady, The, quoted, 267

Sandra Belloni, quoted, 90, 91, 92, 94, 135, 148, 150, 151, 200, 213, 252, 253, 254, 267, 268, 281

INDEX

Sanity, 75 ; definition of, 23
Sculpture, Greek, 8
Seed Time, quoted, 77
Sentimentalism and egoism, 218 *et seq.*
Shakespeare, William, 38, 54, 266, 275, 286, 295, 302
Sharp, Mr. William, 119
Shaving of Shagpat, The, quoted, 207, 267, 268
Shelley, Percy Bysshe, 30, 58, 60, 266, 289
South West Wind in the Woodland, quoted, 70
Spirit of Shakespeare, The, quoted, 257, 302
Star Sirius, The, quoted, 92
Stevenson, Robert Louis, 60, 274
Style, Detachment of, in some writers, 298

Tennyson, Alfred, 276
Test of Manhood, The, quoted, 68, 72
Thomson, James, 52, 165 (quoted)
Thrush in February, The, quoted, 79
Tragedy, 164 *et seq.* ; optimism in the face of, 183

Tragic Comedians, The, quoted, 85, 125, 200, 262, 270
Trevelyan, Mr. G. M., 43, 58, 61 (quoted)
Trifling, Canker of perpetual, 115
Turgenieff, Ivan, 1 *n.*, 82, 208, 289, 298
Types, Novelist of, 7 *et seq.*

Vittoria, quoted, 90, 168, 270, 278

Whitman, Walt, 50, 82, 163, 188, 189, 192 (quoted), 274, 289
Wit and aphorism, Difference between, 259
Women, Position of, 112 *et seq.*
Woodland Peace, quoted, 66
Woods of Westermain, The, quoted, 79
Words, Use of, 37
Wordsworth, William, 36

Young Princess, The, quoted, 95

Y